Trivia
CROSSWORDS
TO KEEP YOU SHARP

STANLEY NEWMAN

PUZZLE
WRIGHT
PRESS

An imprint of Sterling
Publishing Co., Inc.
www.puzzlewright.com

Puzzlewright Press and the distinctive Puzzlewright Press logo are registered trademarks of
Sterling Publishing Co., Inc.

AARP Books include a wide range of titles on
health, personal finance, lifestyle, and other
subjects to enrich the lives of 50+ Americans.

For more information, go to www.aarp.org/books

AARP, established in 1958, is a nonprofit, nonpartisan organization
with more than 40 million members age 50 and older. The views
expressed herein do not necessarily represent the policies of AARP
and should not be construed as endorsements.

The AARP name and logo are registered trademarks of AARP,
used under license to Sterling Publishing Co., Inc.

4   6   8   10   9   7   5   3

Published by Sterling Publishing Co., Inc.
387 Park Avenue South, New York, NY 10016
© 2009 by Stanley Newman
These puzzles originally appeared in
Stanley Newman's Ultimate Trivia Crosswords Volume 1
© 2003 by Stanley Newman
Distributed in Canada by Sterling Publishing
c/o Canadian Manda Group, 165 Dufferin Street
Toronto, Ontario, Canada M6K 3H6
Distributed in the United Kingdom by GMC Distribution Services
Castle Place, 166 High Street, Lewes, East Sussex, England BN7 1XU
Distributed in Australia by Capricorn Link (Australia) Pty. Ltd.
P.O. Box 704, Windsor, NSW 2756, Australia

Sterling ISBN 978-1-4027-6376-2

For information about custom editions, special sales, premium and
corporate purchases, please contact Sterling Special Sales
Department at 800-805-5489 or specialsales@sterlingpublishing.com.

Contents

Introduction

Welcome to *Trivia Crosswords to Keep You Sharp*, featuring the most trivia-packed puzzles ever published.

If you're familiar with the puzzles that I create and edit, you already know that they are sprinkled with a wide variety of factual information from many fields. For this series, that usual sprinkling has been increased to a much higher level. To start with, each of the 50 crosswords herein has a theme based on material from *15,003 Answers: The Ultimate Trivia Encyclopedia*, which I cowrote with Hal Fittipaldi. Beyond the themes, you will find a high percentage of clues and answers that will test your trivia knowledge rather than your vocabulary. To accomplish this, it was necessary to construct these puzzles much differently from the usual—selecting as many answers as possible that would lend themselves to factual clues. This was no doubt as much of a trivia challenge as you will have in solving the puzzles.

For their help in the preparation of this book, I would like to thank Peter Gordon, my Puzzlewright editor, as well as Patrick Blindauer and Amy Reynaldo, for their thorough proofreading of the manuscript. Your comments on any aspect of this book are most welcome. You can reach me via regular mail at the address below. If you're Internet-active, you can reach me electronically through my Web site: www.StanXwords.com, which features prize contests, puzzlemaker profiles, solving hints and other fun stuff for crossword fans. Please drop by for a visit.

Best wishes for happy solving!

—Stan Newman
P.O. Box 2
Boca Raton, FL 33497
(Please enclose a self-addressed,
stamped envelope if you'd like a reply)

Satchel Paige's "How to Stay Young"

Another rule: "Keep the juices flowing by jangling around gently as you move."

ACROSS

1 Macaroni shape
6 Cornell's home
12 Part of a French play
16 Transparent fabric
17 One of six in a Nixon book
18 Installed, as carpeting
19 "If your stomach disputes you, lie down and pacify it with ___"
21 One of the Brady kids
22 Site of Vulcan's forge
23 "Kitten ___ Keys"
24 Madison vice president Elbridge
25 WJM anchorman
26 Seaweed-wrapped fish
27 Like Wes Craven films
29 What Brits call potato chips
31 Suppress
33 Comic Kabibble
36 Build
39 Composer of Johnny Carson's theme
41 Fox, in *Back to the Future*
44 Cribbage pieces
46 Edmund Hillary's guide Tenzing ___
47 Square mile fraction
48 "Avoid ___ at all times"
50 Lavish affection
51 Memorable Billie Burke role
53 German auto
54 '30s president of Czechoslovakia
55 *Our Miss Brooks* star
57 Nicolas Cage is one in *Raising Arizona*
59 Tom Sawyer's half-brother
60 Pricey coffee
62 Monopoly pieces
66 Ben Stiller's mom
68 New Age surroundings
71 Patsy
72 One of the Corleone brothers
74 First woman member of Parliament
75 Periodic table stat.
76 Mutual fund sales charge
77 "___. Something might be gaining on you"
80 Kin of contra-
81 Sneaker hole
82 One taught one-to-one
83 Army outpost
84 Irving Berlin waltz
85 Violinist who helped save Carnegie Hall

DOWN

1 "You get the idea ..."
2 Post-riot felon
3 1988 Summer Olympics hero
4 ___ podrida
5 Drenched
6 Windows screen pictures
7 Consequences alternative
8 Mensa entrance requirement
9 *A Hard Road to Glory* author
10 Op. ___ (footnote abbr.)
11 Balaam's beast
12 Rags-to-riches author
13 "Go very light on the vices, such as ___ in society"
14 Management level
15 Tense
20 Hanover or Plantagenet
24 Paul Masson competitor
26 Agile
27 Bering, for one
28 Adhered
30 Jennifer Lopez role
32 Optimistic assessment
34 Bladed shoe
35 Roy Rogers sidekick
37 "Brain" of a computer
38 One with a lease
40 Fervid
41 Sorcerers
42 II to the VIIIth power
43 "Avoid ___ which angry up the blood"
45 African antelope
48 WWII Allies' tool
49 Put the kibosh on
52 Tony Randall title role of '64
54 Greetings for the villain
56 Greek letter
58 Xavier Cugat ex
61 *Chico and the Man* setting
63 Kane's Xanadu, for example
64 JFK's Secret Service code name
65 Oral
67 Wally Cleaver's pal
69 Onetime *Meet the Press* moderator
70 Alex Haley bestseller
72 Bodybuilder's bane
73 Author Jaffe
74 All over again
75 Touch up against
77 Narcs' agcy.
78 Toon with a 14AAAAAA shoe
79 Round Table regulars: Abbr.

ANSWER, PAGE 56

328
2
———
656

Capital Rivers

Others include Oklahoma City (on the North Canadian River)
and Des Moines (on the Des Moines River).

ACROSS

1 Zodiac sign
6 *Upstairs, Downstairs* star
11 Explosive initials
14 Diarist Nin
15 10-point type
16 "It Had to Be ___"
17 CCCXXVIII doubled
18 Sternness
19 Odysseus, to Laertes
20 State capital on the Willamette River
22 *A Chorus Line* finale
23 ___-poly
24 *Mad* founder William
26 "Oh, ___!" (Austin Powers catchphrase)
29 Without ___ (broke)
31 Hole in one
32 Prefix for nautical

34 Painter of ballet scenes
38 State capital on Crow Creek
42 "High ___" (Sinatra tune)
43 Korean border river
44 Skim milk's lack
45 Gillette razors
47 Barney Fife portrayer
50 Jed Clampett's nephew
53 Daytime drama
54 Stowe character Little ___
55 State capital on the Colorado River
61 Vietnam Veterans Memorial designer
62 Color of Libya's flag
63 Like argon

64 Fall behind
65 Approving of
66 Corruptible
67 John Lennon's adopted middle name
68 Robins' residences
69 One of the Muses

DOWN

1 Young fellows
2 ___ *Gold* (Cussler novel)
3 Lucie Arnaz's mom
4 Frida Kahlo's husband
5 *I, Robot* author
6 Joyful
7 "I cannot tell ___"
8 TV's Emma Peel
9 Curly or Shemp

10 He has a "Hideaway" in *The Pajama Game*
11 Youngest-ever heavyweight boxing champ
12 Herman's Hermits leader
13 *Billboard* chart entries
21 New York city
25 Agenda entry
26 Composer who had 20 children
27 Reverberate
28 Dickensian clerk
29 Fields of expertise
30 Part of Batman's costume
33 New Age vocalist
35 "Forfeit one ___" (Concentration card)

36 Med. school course
37 Preston's peers: Abbr.
39 Slangy agreement
40 *Waiting for Godot* character
41 Preston's domain
46 *Fantasy Island* host
48 Hardy returnee
49 Kitchen device
50 Longtime sponsor of Jack Benny's radio show
51 Perrier competitor
52 "The Rain in Spain," for example
53 Emulates 33-Down
56 Six, in Seville
57 Desert dwelling
58 Lucy Lawless TV role
59 Smell ___ (be suspicious)
60 Battle site of 1944

ANSWER, PAGE 58

Novel Subtitles

Others include *Vanity Fair*: "A Novel Without a Hero"
and *Frankenstein*: "The Modern Prometheus."

ACROSS

1 Indiana Jones quest
6 What the Girl from Ipanema is compared to
11 ___ *Entertainment!*
16 Vishnu worshiper
17 Early computer
18 Word starter meaning "sun"
19 "A Legend of Man's Hunger in His Youth"
22 Suffix for glob
23 Least occupied
24 Moon-shaped
25 Abate
27 Fifth-century pope
29 Author Hubbard
30 Piccadilly Circus statue
32 Philip Nolan's fate
34 "The Parish Boy's Progress"
39 Sty sounds
43 Susan Lucci character
44 Typewriter settings
45 The film world
46 Part of NATO
47 NBC Olympic sportscaster
50 Owns
51 Frisbee inspiration
53 *Lawrence of Arabia* director
54 Makes a mistake

55 Big name in chips
56 "The Autobiography of a Horse"
59 Miss America crown
61 Snakelike fish
62 Sow's mate
65 John Wayne film of '53
68 Company named for an antelope
72 Moss Hart autobiography
74 Taxonomic classifications
76 French article
77 "The Contemplative Man's Recreation"
80 Estrada et al.
81 Eagle's nest
82 E. Power Biggs's instrument

83 One of a corporeal quintet
84 Austin Powers portrayer
85 Film holders

DOWN

1 Halloween costume
2 Cavalry weapon
3 Pennies, often
4 Dictator Amin
5 Movie-camera pioneers' surname
6 Notary need
7 Queen ___ lace (wild carrot)
8 Core
9 Antietam and Actium
10 German exclamation
11 Shortened preposition

12 *Stranger in a Strange Land* author
13 Finnish architect Aalto
14 Make a connection
15 Onetime MTV reporter Tabitha
20 Emmy role for Art Carney
21 *The Time Machine* race
26 PGA Tour nickname
28 Business card abbreviation
31 Movie-within-a-movie in *Scream 2*
33 *Daily Planet* reporter Lane
34 Giraffe relative
35 Source for more than half of English

36 Arm of the sea
37 Boxing org.
38 Fictional setting of the *87th Precinct* novels
40 First prime minister of India
41 Target competitor
42 Sarah Vaughan nickname
45 Australia's capital
47 *Road* picture destination
48 Agcy. first headed by Joseph Kennedy
49 Withstand
52 '70s fad
54 Life of Riley
56 Buddy
57 CIA's headquarters
58 *Green Acres* cow
60 "Excuse me!"
62 High school setting of *Carrie*
63 Painter's pigment
64 Had leftovers, perhaps
66 Steel plow inventor
67 Radio studio sign
69 Protrusion
70 Shaq's last name
71 *Growing Pains* star
73 Wine's aroma
75 French summers
78 Shriver of tennis
79 Coll. senior's exam

ANSWER, PAGE 60

Olive Sizes

Others include Brilliant (291–320 per kilogram)
and Super 38-Across (91–100 per kilogram).

ACROSS
1 Kindergarten lesson
5 "Mighty ___ a Rose"
8 351–380 olives per kilogram
14 *Leadership* author
16 Punish by fine
17 121–140 olives per kilogram
18 What a rock band might go on
19 Fashion monogram
20 Bee weapons
22 Clouseau's rank: Abbr.
23 *Yours, Mine and ___* ('68 film)
24 One ___ (old ball game)
26 Sierra Leone neighbor
29 England personified

33 Role for Shirley
34 Mr. Roberts's first name
36 *Out of Africa* setting
37 River island
38 101–110 olives per kilogram
40 One in charge: Abbr.
41 British poet Tate
43 Up to snuff
44 Ladder step
45 Anna Paquin's Oscar film
47 Break a rule, in bridge
49 French poodle name
50 Rita Coolidge ex
51 World leader born in Kiev
54 Bernese Alps resort

56 Winter bug
59 A predecessor of 14-Across
61 261–290 olives per kilogram
63 It may be hidden
64 Golf tourney twosomes
65 Spruce up
66 Avarice or envy
67 Phoenix suburb

DOWN
1 CIA, e.g.
2 Tell-alls, often
3 Glean
4 Highway warning
5 Fellini Oscar film
6 *Henry and June* character
7 Pottery oven
8 Lomb's partner
9 Sounds of hesitation

10 #1 song of 1970
11 Author Hubbard
12 Onetime French coins
13 39-Down, for short
15 Debate subject
21 High power of 10
23 *Off ___ Comet* (Verne novel)
25 Egyptian symbol of life
26 141–160 olives per kilogram
27 Husband of Bathsheba
28 "___ Last of the Red Hot Mamas" (Sophie Tucker tune)
29 181–200 olives per kilogram
30 Excessive

31 Not playing it straight
32 231–260 olives per kilogram
35 Certain sultan's subjects
38 When *Die Another Day* premiered
39 Maryland athlete
42 Bill Mauldin book
44 Hosp. workers
46 Hunting dog
48 Down source
50 Hawaii's "Garden Isle"
51 Statistical average
52 Margin
53 Denmark-based retail chain
55 Recipe amts.
56 321–350 olives per kilogram
57 Fire fodder
58 Astronomical bear
60 Alphabetic trio
62 Margin

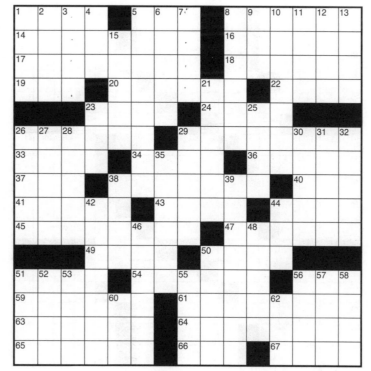

ANSWER, PAGE 62

"We Are the World" Participants

Others include Kim Carnes, Bob Dylan, Bette Midler, and Smokey Robinson.

ACROSS

1 Fancy watch brand
6 Sergeant Friday's desire
11 Opted for
16 Poet/playwright who became a president
17 10/31 option
18 Doozies
19 '70s White House dog
20 "We Are the World" participant
22 "Beetle Bailey" bulldog
23 Pesky insects
24 He's had eight Oscar nominations but has never won
25 "We Are the World" participant
27 Acad. or coll.
28 Thesaurus entry: Abbr.
29 West Coast airport code
30 Lieutenant Sulu portrayer
32 Tony Bennett specialty
36 Pluvious
38 Town near Caen
42 Mr. T's onetime group
43 Composer Prokofiev
44 Frost
45 "We Are the World" participant

48 Coal carriers
49 Be serious
50 Bogart's *Key* ___
51 Otherwise
52 When summers end: Abbr.
53 Eisenhower Supreme Court appointee
54 Allergen, at times
56 Where the ilium is
57 Ken Burns's network
60 Treasury Dept. agency
61 "We Are the World" participant
67 Comparatively steamed
69 Past the deadline
70 Persian spirit

71 "We Are the World" participant
73 "Greece" is pronounced with one
74 Overmuch
75 Hersey novel setting
76 Let loose
77 French states
78 Not italic
79 Maid of '60s TV

DOWN

1 George Burns film
2 Cuban national hero
3 Lloyd Webber score
4 Entrain
5 Hirt and Hirschfeld
6 Ky. stronghold

7 Vicinities
8 Word on a nickel
9 Prepares leather
10 Slovenly place
11 Provide with duds
12 Sci-fi literary award
13 Butter substitutes
14 Ill-tempered
15 Krupp Works home
21 Film sequel of '79
23 Homecoming attendee
26 San Antonio shrine
27 Most sensible
30 Baghdad's river
31 Babylonian love goddess
32 Soak in the tub
33 Playwright Fugard

34 Yorkshire city
35 Leaves the straight and narrow
36 Record again
37 Do not exist
39 "___ is human ..."
40 T-shirt specification
41 Mork's superior
43 Angry looks
46 Brenda Lee tune of '80
47 Reactions to rudeness
53 Shrewd
55 Reese's ___
56 Sherlock Holmes's landlady
57 Vex
58 Main impact
59 "You ___ mouthful!"
61 International airline of yore
62 *In the* ___ (Nixon book)
63 '50s toothpaste
64 Lucy Ricardo's landlady
65 "Live Free ___" (New Hampshire motto)
66 Basil's frequent costar
68 Type of bolt attachment
69 Fuss
72 It holds the mayo
73 "What was that?"

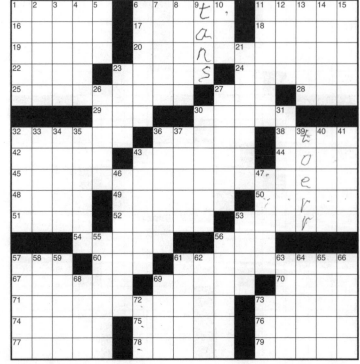

ANSWER, PAGE 64

Howdy Doody

Nonspeaking clown Clarabell Hornblow was first portrayed by Bob Keeshan, who would later become Captain Kangaroo.

ACROSS

1 Keep an eye on
5 Accouterments
9 Last Soviet first lady
14 George Sand, to Chopin
15 Forearm bone
16 British Derby site
17 Princess Summerfall Winterspring belonged to it
20 The Orioles' division
21 Spanish muralist
22 Employee ID, often
23 Schubert song
25 Job opening
27 Eight-animals-in-one puppet
31 Senate Watergate Committee member
35 Poetic adverb
36 Joplin compositions
38 Eldest of the Cartwright boys
39 One of Hamlet's choices
41 Bowling center units
42 *The Persistence of Memory* painter
43 ___ instant (quickly)
44 Useful facts
45 Novels and such, for short
46 *Meet the Parents* dad's portrayer
48 Howdy Doody had 48 of them
52 Slips into
54 Snarl
55 High bond rating
58 Parcel (out)
60 Belmont Stakes winner in '75
64 The voice of Howdy Doody
67 Scarecrow's desire
68 "You've got ___!"
69 Diminutive suffix
70 They come in skeins
71 WWII journalist
72 Barrett of gossip

DOWN

1 Brit's farewell
2 First Best Actor Oscar winner Jannings
3 Musical based on 8½
4 American Revolution general from Germany
5 Plundered
6 "Don't Bring Me Down" rock group
7 Jillian et al.
8 *The ___ Progress* (Stravinsky opera)
9 1984 Summer Olympics star
10 Truth in Lending stat.
11 Egyptian goddess
12 Weeps audibly
13 Sherman Hemsley sitcom
18 Land east of the Urals
19 1930 Oscar winner as Disraeli
24 Sugar Ray Leonard victim in '80
26 *The Wind in the Willows* character
27 Foul-smelling
28 Spaghetti western director
29 Name of eight popes
30 Canadian Rockies resort
32 JFK cabinet member Stewart
33 Ivy Leaguer
34 Gives off
37 Conductor Solti
40 Oklahoma city
41 Middle name of toy electric train inventor Joshua Cowen
47 New Testament epistle
49 Make possible
50 Cleveland cagers, familiarly
51 *Seinfeld* character
53 "King Porter ___" (Jelly Roll Morton tune)
55 Big name in advice
56 Subtle atmosphere
57 From a distance
59 Internet auction giant
61 Jackson 5 brother
62 Envelope abbreviation
63 Second-largest living bird
65 Prominent feature of some '50s autos
66 J.R. Ewing commodity

ANSWER, PAGE 56

11

Occupation Surnames

Others include "Hayward" (fence inspector),
"Harper" (minstrel), and "Collier" (coal miner).

ACROSS

1 Rechargable battery
6 Georgia city
11 *Bringing Up Baby* director
16 In unison
17 Area of fruit trees
18 South American plain
19 What "Chandler" means
21 Old Testament prophet
22 Element discovered by Marie Curie
23 What "Fowler" means
25 *The Name of the Rose* author
26 ___ *Macabre*
28 Karl Marx collaborator
29 Declare untrue
30 Swell, to a rapper
32 Wimbledon champ in '75
35 Its ticker symbol is X
38 Stop up
42 What Hepburn called Tracy
44 Sharer's pronoun
45 Author Binchy
46 What "Tinker" means
49 *Boléro* composer
50 ___ B'rith
51 Subject of a will
52 Court hearing

53 Guy Lombardo's real first name
55 Sodium hydroxide solutions
56 Loni Anderson ex
57 Altar neighbor
59 Bogart film of '43
63 Camera setting
65 Popular dog breed, for short
68 What "Dyker" means
71 *Annie Hall* catchphrase
73 *Sanford and Son* character
74 What "Carter" means
76 ___ Haute, Indiana
77 First Spanish month
78 Cotton fabric
79 Meal with matzoh

80 "You Make Me Feel Like Dancing" singer
81 Where the world's highest volcano is

DOWN

1 Mother-of-pearl source
2 *Love Boat* bartender
3 Tenant-owned apartment
4 *The King* ___
5 Fool
6 *The Band Wagon* studio
7 Some OPEC ministers
8 Telejournalist Roberts
9 More than
10 *If I Ran the Zoo* character

11 Texas oil billionaire
12 *Drums ___ the Mohawk*
13 Efficiency expert's bane
14 Prepare to be knighted
15 Flies high
20 ___ Ravelli (Chico Marx in *Animal Crackers*)
24 Recuperate
27 Cuomo or Pataki's domain: Abbr.
29 Home of a U.S. Mint
30 Darius's realm
31 "___ real nowhere man"
32 Nolan Ryan, in the '80s
33 Hairdresser's need
34 Lift with difficulty

36 Shakespeare specialty
37 Pull on, as one's ear
38 Chess move
39 Wallace's '68 running mate
40 Roundish
41 Splicing candidates
43 Animation frame
45 French pronoun
47 Construction beam
48 Mozart's father
53 Battleground of 1944
54 William Styron title character
56 Clinton Supreme Court appointee
58 Peloponnesian War winner
59 Army noncoms: Abbr.
60 Up ___ (trapped)
61 Secret stash
62 Mia Farrow ex
63 Old-fashioned sort
64 Saw logs
65 Much more than miffed
66 *Die Fledermaus* maid
67 Reveals
69 Bowls over
70 Capital of Yemen
72 "Runaround Sue" singer
75 "... ___ a lender be"

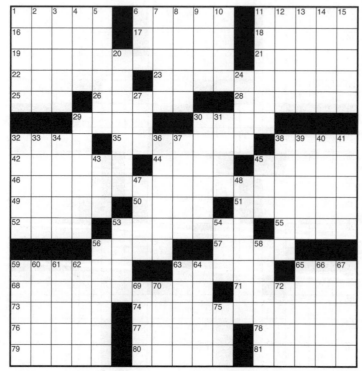

ANSWER, PAGE 58

The Liberty Bell

The 2,080-pound Liberty Bell was stored in 11-Down's
Zion High German Reformed Church during the American Revolution.

ACROSS

1 Puccini opera
6 Final Four round
11 Mont Blanc, for example
14 Wee hour
15 A deadly sin
16 Antietam general
17 Misspelled word on the Liberty Bell
19 First U.N. Secretary-General Trygve ___
20 Top of the head
21 Gehrig or Mantle, for short
22 Former president of NOW
24 One of the Mercury astronauts
26 Father of Rosemary's baby
28 *Three Men ___ Baby*
30 American Red Cross founder
33 *Amazing Stories* and *Fantastic Adventures*, familiarly
37 Suffix for method
39 What Dr Pepper isn't
40 GM European car
41 As the script indicates
42 ___ *a Teen-age Werewolf*
43 PBS science series
44 Mediocre report card
45 Where Tsavo National Park is
46 Whoville meanie
48 JFK's rank in *PT 109*
50 Annoy
52 *Erin Brockovich* Oscar winner
57 Macon breakfast
59 Reebok rival
61 *Truth or ___* (Madonna documentary)
62 NRC predecessor
63 Pair who cast the Liberty Bell
66 Baton Rouge sch.
67 Sir ___ John
68 *Still Me* author
69 Aliens, for short
70 Talks hoarsely
71 First African-American golfer to play in the Masters

DOWN

1 Big name in baseball cards
2 Either of two *Paper Moon* stars
3 Actress Berger
4 Mudville slugger
5 One of the March girls
6 Philo Vance creator
7 Enthusiasm
8 Religious recluses
9 "Like ___ *love* it!"
10 Cascade Range peak
11 Where the Liberty Bell was once stored
12 Luke's sister
13 Thurman, in *The Avengers*
18 Lolita star Sue
23 She calls Peppermint Patty "Sir"
25 Profs.' aides
27 Competent
29 Faster, in mus.
31 Oil of ___
32 *The Right Stuff* agency
33 '70s video game
34 "Put ___ shut ..."
35 Source of the Biblical quote on the Liberty Bell
36 Krypton or Melmac
38 Mozart and Schwarzenegger, by birth
41 Protest singer Phil
45 Soviet spy org.
47 Comics ghost
49 Benoit or Crawford
51 Bridge seats
53 Car with a Teletouch transmission
54 Did a reviewer's job
55 Treasure source
56 Ed Norton's workplace
57 Dorothy's last name in *The Wizard of Oz*
58 Take it easy
60 Letters on cognac bottles
64 Words before carte or king
65 Dr. of rap

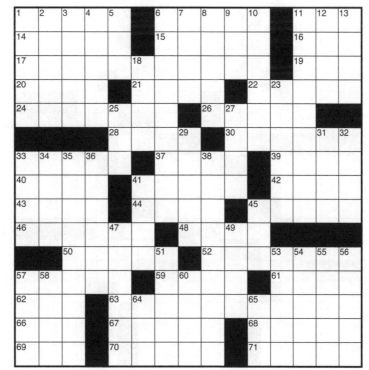

ANSWER, PAGE 60

Unlikely Singers in Films

Others include Clint Eastwood ("I Talk to the Trees" in *Paint Your Wagon*) and Warren Beatty and Dustin Hoffman ("That's Amore" in *Ishtar*).

ACROSS

1 ___ point (.0001, on Wall Street)
6 Silents actress Banky
11 Burt Reynolds's *Gunsmoke* role
16 Fowl place
17 Bygone toymaker
18 *Lorenzo's Oil* star
19 Synthetic fiber
20 "Pretty Irish Girl" in *Darby O'Gill and the Little People*
22 "Up and ___!"
23 Sonora snoozes
24 Citrus drinks
25 Lerner & Loewe score
27 Jim Varney character
29 "Red River Valley" in *The Grapes of Wrath*
31 Baseball great Combs
35 ___ a soul (no one)
36 Fitness center
38 John, in Scotland
39 Edgar or Hugo
43 Morty, in *Northern Exposure*
46 Boric or nitric
47 "Too Close to Paradise" in *Paradise Alley*
51 *Tres* times *dos*
52 Andy, on *Taxi*
53 King Arthur's father
54 Catchall abbr.
55 Adjective for the Beatles

56 Shimmier of song
59 Lost dog in an Inge play
61 "Puttin' on the Ritz" in *Idiot's Delight*
67 Sheep sounds
70 Minnie, in a Cab Calloway tune
71 Shock jock Don
74 Chinese checkers needs
76 "Dolphin-safe" fish
77 "Bing! Bang! Bong!" in *Houseboat*
79 Classic comedy actress ZaSu
80 Previous
81 Nicholas Gage book
82 Comic Fields
83 *Fiddler on the Roof* matchmaker
84 *Giant* ranch

85 "There was ___ woman who lived ..."

DOWN

1 Bring up, as a subject
2 Major arteries
3 Serious
4 Variant compound
5 Depot: Abbr.
6 One booed at the ballpark
7 Notion, in Nantes
8 Like some office equipment
9 Chanter's syllables
10 Highway from Fairbanks to British Columbia
11 Fay Wray, in *King Kong*
12 Mozart piece

13 Made a court statement
14 To be: French
15 Alejandro and Fernando
21 Suffix meaning "sugar"
23 Settee relative
26 He introduced "Kids" in *Bye Bye Birdie*
28 Where buoy meets gull
30 Shea Stadium player, once
32 Japanese copier company
33 Singer of the *Rawhide* theme
34 Orson Scott Card title character
36 Mach 2 flier
37 Potpie veggie
39 Beasts of burden

40 *Christina's World* painter
41 Waitress at Mel's
42 Trailer park occupants
44 Where "nanu-nanu" is spoken
45 Japanese port
46 Keyboard key
48 Cinque once headed it: Abbr.
49 Keyboard key
50 "¡Hasta ___!"
55 Transportation Dept. agency
57 Where Yerevan is capital
58 Refs' decisions
60 Air-gun pellet
61 King of pop music
62 L.A. tar pit site
63 Comic book in which Superman first appeared
64 Former prime minister of Pakistan
65 Soup legume
66 Wiped clean
68 Drs.' lobby
69 Farm machine
71 '60s secret agent TV show
72 Magazine for women over 40
73 ___ arms (agitated)
75 Penitential period
78 Fury
79 Bake sale org.

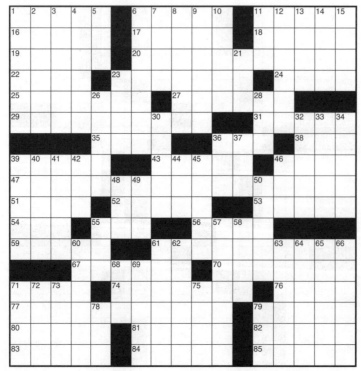

ANSWER, PAGE 62

eBay Prohibited Items

Others include fireworks, lottery tickets, and postage meters.

ACROSS

1 "Mm! Mm! ___!" (Campbell's slogan)
5 Judy Garland's real last name
9 "Waterloo" group
13 *The Egg* ___
14 Phrase of understanding
15 France, to Caesar
16 eBay prohibited items
19 Friend of Buckwheat
20 Hard work
21 Con game
23 Parton/Ronstadt/ Harris album
25 Mongrel
27 U.N. Day month
28 eBay prohibited items
32 Author Deighton
33 Igneous rock source
34 Toy merchant Schwarz
35 Do a gumshoe's job
37 Political pamphlet
39 Academic periods: Abbr.
41 College major, for short
44 Russian refusal
46 Monogram part: Abbr.
48 *All in the Family* producer
49 Open-mouth sound
51 eBay prohibited items
54 Winter bug
55 Popular success
56 Inert gas
57 Father of instant photography
59 Hoodlum
61 More peculiar
65 eBay prohibited items
68 Quarterback who became a congressman
69 Author Dinesen
70 Pro ___ (proportionally)
71 Mars's alias
72 Small islands
73 Ollie's partner

DOWN

1 Sound of fright
2 "___ bigger and better things!"
3 Scent
4 Warren Beatty film role
5 USO show attendees
6 "The Nation's Newspaper"
7 *Send ___ Flowers* (Day/Hudson film)
8 Florentine VIP of old
9 In the past
10 Makes illegal
11 First *To Tell the Truth* host
12 Lorraine's neighbor
17 Actress Sedgwick
18 Like a foil's point
22 Any of the Sierras: Abbr.
24 *Concerto* ___ (Gershwin work)
26 Gather grain
28 Sandwich order
29 Dumbo's wing
30 *The Blackboard Jungle* author
31 Pulitzer's New York paper
36 Stanley Cup champs, 1980–83
38 Engineering school, for short
40 Corvette model
42 George Sanders screen persona
43 Barry Bonds stat
45 Overused
47 Numbered rd.
49 CIO partner
50 Popular cruise destination
52 Like some cuisine
53 Henhouse
58 Capitol feature
60 "___ daisy!"
62 W.C. Fields exclamation
63 Sundance's girlfriend
64 Granny on *The Beverly Hillbillies*
66 Record label sites
67 Approves

ANSWER, PAGE 64

Kennedy Center Honorees

Others include Richard Rodgers (1978),
Lucille Ball (1986), and Clint Eastwood (2000).

ACROSS

1 Pencil puzzles
6 2,650, to Tacitus
11 Resided
16 John Ronald ___ Tolkien
17 Olds model
18 Taxonomic classification
19 Director (1990)
21 Paul Anka tune
22 Markers
23 Creative bunch
25 Site of a Popeye tattoo
26 Astronaut Grissom
27 Sportscaster shout
28 Singer (1984)
31 Cub Scout group
32 Kramden's workplace
33 Repair
34 Separated
37 *Angela's Ashes* sequel
38 *Judgment at Nuremberg* actor
41 Frosted Flakes tiger
42 ___ Lingus
43 Singer/songwriter (1997)
44 Antediluvian
45 ___ the Impaler (Dracula inspirer)
46 *"Vesti la giubba"* is one
47 A/C unit
48 Actress (1988)
50 2002 Winter Olympics host
51 Iambs and spondees
52 Angler, at times
53 "The ___ of Aquarius"
54 Reagan cabinet member
55 Bluenose
56 SMU or USC
57 Richard Pryor title role
58 Actor (1981)
61 *Invasion of the Body Snatchers* "cocoon"
62 Website info, for short
65 ___ out a living
66 Spanish sherry
68 *Laverne and Shirley* character Carmine "The Big ___"
69 *The Sopranos* matriarch
72 Dancer/actor (1978)
74 Sevareid et al.
75 Have another session
76 Toon coyote
77 "Mr. Cub"
78 Road curves
79 *Superman* cub reporter

DOWN

1 Boris Badenov's boss
2 Vowel sequence
3 South African people
4 Sushi bar offerings
5 Family Stone head
6 "And pretty ___ all in a row"
7 Fr. miss
8 James Joyce hero
9 Some liqueurs
10 *Two Women* star
11 One of the DiMaggio brothers
12 Like some senses of humor
13 Playwright (1996)
14 Live's partner
15 Solicitous phrase
20 Vienna, in Vienna
24 German Southwest Africa, today
27 To date
29 Louella's rival
30 Start of the Boy Scout Oath
31 Sec
32 Matthew Modine film of '84
34 They may get smashed
35 Octopus or cuttlefish
36 Conductor (1998)
37 *Coffee, ___ Me?*
38 Not as good
39 Hotel door posting
40 Coach Rockne
42 Fast tempo
43 "Slinging Sammy" of football
45 Brazilian airline
49 Not any
51 *Casablanca* headgear
53 Sean Young or Glenn Close
54 Prefix for year
56 Night noises
57 Pursues romantically
58 Gossip column subject
59 Director Kurosawa
60 Woodard of *Cross Creek*
61 H.S. jrs.' exams
62 Comes up short
63 *Hollywood Squares* response
64 Dannay/Lee sleuth
67 "Garfield" dog
68 Racetrack boundary
70 "That's disgusting!"
71 Ornery equine
73 Early afternoon

ANSWER, PAGE 56

Superman

There is a museum devoted to Superman
in the aptly named Metropolis, Illinois.

ACROSS

1 "Soon to be a ___ motion picture"
6 Columnist Joseph
11 Denver clock setting: Abbr.
14 *Call Me ___* (Bob Hope film of '63)
15 Allow to pass
16 Letter after pi
17 With 59-Across, *Daily Planet* motto
19 Pie ingredient?
20 Draft org.
21 Light wood
22 Cast a spell on
24 Daughter of Ming the Merciless
25 Milk farm
27 *Hogan's Heroes* star
31 Weissmuller role
34 ALF or Mork
35 Cape Cod formations
37 Post- opposite
38 18-wheelers
39 Element #5
40 Alphabetic quartet
41 She played Marlon's girlfriend in *On the Waterfront*

42 Feudal estate
43 "___ of the Ball" (Leroy Anderson piece)
44 Roll back
46 '70s fad runner
48 *Gorky Park* detective Arkady
50 Emcee
51 Casio competitor
53 Sets one back
55 Tallahassee sch.
58 Soap opera storyline
59 See 17-Across
62 Med. insurance option
63 Project Gemini rocket stage
64 Arthur Miller title character
65 Back muscle, for short
66 Machine part

67 Ogden Nash's "two-l" beast

DOWN

1 Harvard degs.
2 Hole-punching tools
3 007's *Moonraker* foe
4 "Hooked ___ Feeling" ('69 tune)
5 *Match Game* emcee
6 Presidential candidate of '36
7 *Fantasy Island* souvenirs
8 Italian violin, for short
9 No longer in use: Abbr.
10 Mythical fast friend of Damon

11 Superman's fifth dimension foe
12 *Melrose Place* actor Andrew
13 *Around the World in 80 Days* producer Mike
18 Author Paretsky
23 Go wrong
24 Experts
26 "___ o'clock scholar"
27 Less decorated
28 Castor and Nana's daughter, in cartoons
29 Nickname for Metropolis, with "the"
30 They replaced the markka and mark
32 As ___ (generally)
33 "When pigs fly!"

36 Part of Ursa Minor
39 Pitcher's no-no
40 Bicycle part
42 1920 Preakness winner
43 *That Girl* actor Ted
45 "A mouse!"
47 *Goodbye, Columbus* author
49 Twosome times four
51 Political humorist Mort
52 Writer Bombeck
54 "Good heavens!"
55 Govt. disaster aid org.
56 Emulated Spitz
57 Jimmy Carter's alma mater: Abbr.
60 "___ to Extremes" (Billy Joel tune)
61 Former Cambodian leader

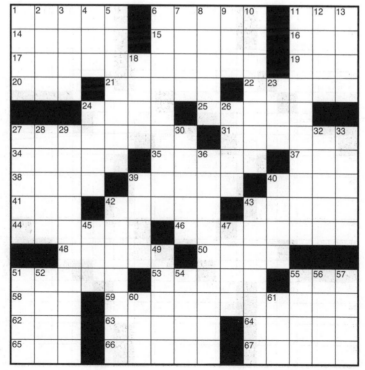

ANSWER, PAGE 58

Sports "Animal" Nicknames

Others include "Raging Bull" (Jack LaMotta),
"Grey Eagle" (Tris Speaker), and "The Bird" (Mark Fidrych).

ACROSS

1 *Oklahoma!* aunt
6 Ted Knight's sitcom wife
11 Honda's home
16 Bushed
17 United competitor
18 Sun Valley's state
19 "Big Dog" of football
21 Leigh's *Psycho* sister
22 Guaranteed winner, in sports
23 Comes up
24 Man, in Cannes
25 Soap ingredient
26 Earns, with "down"
27 Promissory notes
29 Get ___ of one's own medicine
31 Migratory sea bird
32 ___ alai
35 Fred Flintstone's boss
36 Suffix meaning "sort of"
38 Makes mad
40 Small city
41 With 50-Across, "Spider" of tennis
44 Roast host
45 How some tuna is packed
47 In the future
48 Farmer, at times

49 Certain sculpture
50 See 41-Across
52 Concerning
53 Gielgud's Oscar film
55 Forty winks
56 Onetime immigration island
58 Slangy refusal
59 Nerd
61 Anglican Church offshoot: Abbr.
62 Diddy's real first name
63 New ___, India
65 *The Wizard of Oz* setting: Abbr.
68 *The Bell Jar* writer
71 Be precariously perched
73 Model Macpherson
74 He makes you mad
75 "Goose" of football

77 JFK Library architect
78 With pasta, in product names
79 Troop group
80 First name of *The Rookies* actor Brown
81 Reform Party founder
82 Pothook shapes

DOWN

1 *The Seven Year Itch* star
2 Baby ___ (W.C. Fields foil)
3 "Bambi" of football
4 Aviator Lindbergh
5 Sandwich bread
6 English Channel swimmer of '26
7 Author Shute

8 *Cagney & Lacey* star
9 Raison d'___
10 Dog star
11 "Catfish" of baseball
12 Lone Ranger's farewell
13 Something to read
14 Throat-clearing sound
15 Jamie Farr's outstanding feature
20 Sartre novel
26 Poker prize
28 Hosp. areas
30 Like Niels Bohr
31 Warbucks henchman
32 "Golden Bear" of golf
33 Mideast rulers: Var.

34 French ship that brought the Statue of Liberty to the U.S.
35 Mexican state
36 Start of a Descartes quote
37 Old Testament queendom
39 Paperless messages
40 Tennessee NFLer
42 Fall back
43 Ruckus
46 "Iron Horse" of baseball
51 Word form for "kidney"
54 *The Crying Game* star
57 Half of CIV
60 Capture
61 Latin for "he has chosen"
62 *Rawhide* beast
63 Room furnishings
64 It means "race"
66 Seaweed
67 Must have
68 Puritanical type
69 *The Third Man* villain
70 Dog food endorsed by Lorne Greene
72 Word on Irish stamps
73 Atts.' titles
76 Compass reading

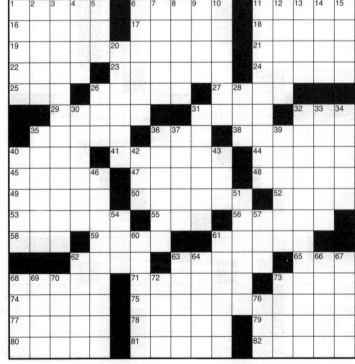

ANSWER, PAGE 60

Bandleader Theme Songs

Others include "Let's Dance" (Benny Goodman), "Moonlight Serenade" (Glenn Miller), and "Bubbles in the Wine" (Lawrence Welk).

ACROSS

1 1989 PGA Player of the Year Tom
5 Last word of the New Testament
9 *Come Back, Little ___*
14 "Cradle of Love" singer Billy
15 March Madness org.
16 *Lost in a ___* (Abbott and Costello film)
17 Union-balloting agcy.
18 Crew team members
19 Head Keebler elf
20 "Apurksody"
22 Mashie and niblick
23 ___-Mart
24 Yvonne's role in *The Munsters*
26 His horse was Diablo

31 Lee of *The Fall Guy*
35 Pizza topping
36 Celebration
38 Carpet calculation
39 "Little" girl of comics
40 Key of Schumann's Third Symphony
41 *Night Court* bailiff portrayer Richard
42 "This ___ outrage!"
43 Rabin predecessor
44 Patron saint of France
45 Crunch maker
47 Ringling Museum of Art locale
49 Like some autos
51 Badminton need
52 Bochco legal series
55 "Nightmare"

61 Got up
62 '90s Teri Hatcher TV role
63 "King of the road"
64 Standard Oil of New York
65 Answering machine sound
66 1952 Winter Olympics site
67 Photographer Adams
68 Eros alias
69 Dandelion, for example

DOWN

1 "Stand by Me" singer
2 Monty Python member
3 *Larry Sanders Show* costar
4 Hamburg's river

5 Arctic jacket
6 General who said "Nuts!" to the Germans
7 O.K. Corral gunfighter
8 Like Fran Drescher's voice
9 Woman, to "Crocodile" Dundee
10 "Ciribiribin"
11 Cube inventor Rubik
12 Hippie happening
13 Singing brothers' surname
21 Tae ___ do
25 "... ___ a man with seven wives"
26 Madeleine's successor
27 Occupied
28 Fictional Marner

29 "One O'Clock Jump"
30 Sandwich shops
32 University of Maine town
33 Ignited again
34 Nacho topping
37 *Pulp Fiction* director
40 NYSE rival
44 Tropical fruit
46 Poet family's surname
48 *Mad About You* star
50 Crimean resort
52 *Lost Horizon* character
53 Elvis ___ Presley
54 Tennis shots
56 *A ___ With a View*
57 Finish third
58 Pale ___ (White Sox)
59 Well-qualified
60 *American Gothic* painter

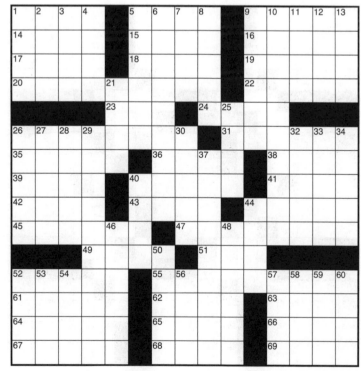

ANSWER, PAGE 62

Centenarians

Others include entertainer Bob Hope (1903–2003), film producer
Hal Roach (1892–1992), and ventriloquist Señor Wences (1896–1999).

ACROSS

1 *The Power of Positive Thinking* author
6 *The Effect of ___ Rays on Man-in-the-Moon Marigolds*
11 Lilliput creator
16 "___ River" (*Show Boat* tune)
17 Trojan War epic
18 Eagle nest
19 Comedian (1896–1996)
21 Peggy Lee tune of '58
22 Siberian city
23 Shakespearean Athenian
24 Swinelike beasts
25 Presidential nickname
26 A ways away
28 PBS "Science Guy"
29 Texas A&M athlete
33 Hasty escape
36 Feeling sorry about
38 Singer on Godfrey's show
40 Puzzles made from hedges
42 Blind as ___
45 Flora
46 ___ cheese dressing
47 Like Nero Wolfe
48 Female lobster
49 Presidential candidate (1887–1987)
52 Alphabetic trio
53 South America's "spine"
55 Rock guitarist Hendrix
56 Two-___ (short film)
58 ___ Club (Costco competitor)
59 Shape of a torus
60 Suit introduced in 1946
61 *Roots* Emmy winner
63 FedEx alternative
65 Periods before Easter
66 Peyton Place's main street
68 "No ifs, ___, or buts!"
70 Be under the weather
72 Neighbor of Ozzie and Harriet
74 Strauss specialty
77 PDQ
81 Mixes it up with
82 Presidential mother (1890–1995)
84 French river
85 Part of NAFTA
86 Chip giant
87 Wholesale quantities
88 Ferber et al.
89 "Common Sense" writer

DOWN

1 Walt Kelly creation
2 K-5
3 *Ben and Me* mouse
4 Escapade
5 Chang's brother
6 Vet's benefit
7 Reunion attendee
8 Spanish painter
9 Divine nourishment
10 Words from the sponsor
11 Swahili for "journey"
12 Emulate Niobe
13 Composer (1888–1989)
14 Like some tempers
15 Of few words
20 Pilot's announcement: Abbr.
24 Greek crosses
25 Jai alai baskets
27 Austrian analyst
29 Constellations' brightest stars
30 Lead ore
31 Painter (1860–1961)
32 Charged particle
34 Spielberg production company
35 *The Fixer* author
37 Run in
39 Gallaudet communication method: Abbr.
41 *Babbitt* setting
43 Agreement
44 Video game invented in Russia
47 Charlie Chaplin in-law
50 Norwegian physical feature
51 Sphere
54 Superman's insignia
57 Supplement, with "out"
59 Disavow
62 Edict city of 1598
64 Kin of croquettes
66 System of values
67 "The Forbidden City"
69 Excalibur, e.g.
71 Verb ending
73 Hard to find
75 Wise ___ owl
76 Mother of Castor and Pollux
77 "Getting to Know You" singer
78 Space-signal monitoring program in *Contact*
79 Gulf bordering the Red Sea
80 Nabors role
82 AAA recommendation
83 Tuck's partner

ANSWER, PAGE 56

Harry Potter

There are 142 staircases at Hogwarts; in addition to 39-Across,
the other three dorms there are Hufflepuff, Ravenclaw, and Slytherin.

ACROSS

1 "March Madness" org.
5 Memorable Valentino role
10 Not quite closed
14 Merit
15 Erstwhile detergent
16 Timber wolf
17 National wizarding newspaper
20 Entanglement
21 Cake part, at times
22 Ultimate degree
23 "The Big ___" (New Orleans)
25 Network owned by Disney
27 *Let a Simile Be Your Umbrella* author
30 Discoverer of the radiation belts around the Earth
35 Adjective suffix
36 First president of the Sierra Club
38 Break off
39 Where Harry Potter lives at Hogwarts

43 Dancer Shearer
44 Exemplar of dullness
45 Bolshevik
46 University of Michigan home
48 Where the buoys are
51 Three: Italian
52 In the center of
53 "Hit the Road, Jack" singer Charles
56 Satirical newspaper, with *The*
59 Thomas Nast target
63 Required reading at Hogwarts
66 West Point team
67 Trio times three
68 Advertising sign

69 Winning margin, at times
70 Fox's *Family Ties* father
71 State bird of Hawaii

DOWN

1 East Coast NBA team
2 "Call Me Irresponsible" lyricist
3 Two-dimensional extent
4 Ambassador Gromyko
5 ___ Lanka
6 Not flat
7 Singer on the *Lord of the Rings* soundtrack
8 Cosby's first prime-time series

9 Sun Myung Moon, by birth
10 Matterhorn, for one
11 Calvin Coolidge's real first name
12 Aid in wrongdoing
13 *Portnoy's Complaint* author
18 Banned fruit-tree spray
19 Actor who was in the original cast of *The Fantasticks*
24 18-wheeler
26 *The People's Choice* dog
27 Sum symbol, in math
28 Moses's spokesman
29 Arrive via air
30 *War and Peace* director King

31 Baseball superstar's nickname
32 ___ Ingalls Wilder
33 Ruhr Valley city
34 Requirements
37 Loosen
40 Lambda Lambda Lambda, in *Revenge of the Nerds*
41 Sinatra ex
42 Capacity
47 *Bugsy* actress
49 Accredit
50 "Fire Chief" of old-time radio
52 Admission fees of a sort
53 *The Longest Day* author Cornelius
54 Prefix for nautical
55 Orange veggies
57 "Take ___ leave it!"
58 Mr. Bill's cry
60 Very wide shoe
61 Prince William alma mater
62 Partake of a feast
64 Scotch alternative
65 Shaker ___, OH

ANSWER, PAGE 58

"Who's on First" Team

All the team members in the routine are present in the puzzle's title and answers. No right fielder is mentioned.

ACROSS

1 The second baseman
5 2,105
9 Quick to learn
12 Zilch
15 Della Street portrayer Barbara
16 *At Random* author
17 New Deal's "Blue Eagle" org.
18 Plastic ___ Band
19 The third baseman
21 Neil Simon nickname
22 Shelley piece
23 One half of the "Who's on First" duo
24 Egg: French
25 The pitcher
27 *Bewitched* character
29 First CinemaScope feature film
31 Only school to win the NCAA and NIT basketball tournaments in the same year
33 *Concentration* conjunction
34 SASEs, for example
37 *Lost in Space* villain
40 Militarize
42 Plane part
45 The catcher
46 *True ___* (Schwarzenegger film)
48 Acts as censor
49 *Ab ___* (from the beginning)
50 The center fielder
52 The left fielder
53 Author of *Couplehood* and *Babyhood*
56 Patron saint of sailors
57 Had leftovers, perhaps
59 '20s–'30s Fords
61 CIA predecessor
62 Flower in a Whitman poem
63 "This little piggie had ___"
64 Film reel holder
66 Eight, in Essen
68 Character in Clue
71 *GoodFellas* star
75 *The Naughty ___* (film in which "Who's on First" is seen)
78 ___-Tass
80 One half of the "Who's on First" duo
81 *Fables in Slang* author

82 "Are you a man ___ mouse?"
83 The shortstop
85 John Ritter's dad
86 Sleep-stage acronym
87 #1 on the Mohs scale
88 Faucet flaw
89 Feedbag morsel
90 Former conscription org.
91 Brat Pack name
92 "___ It Romantic?"

DOWN

1 As
2 Wore
3 Viva voce
4 Prime-time hour
5 *This Is Spiñal Tap* star
6 List of options
7 *Tomb Raider* heroine
8 Amer. Legion alternative
9 Pyrenees land
10 Movie trailer, for instance
11 *"Yo quiero ___"*
12 Queen who wrote *Leap of Faith* in 2003
13 ___-European (English ancestor)
14 MGM cofounder
20 '30s film sleuth Blane
25 Leoni of *Deep Impact*
26 "Walk Away ___" ('66 tune)
28 Numerical prefix
30 Top grossing comedy of the '90s

32 Cole Porter alma mater
35 Sort of stitchery
36 *The Golden Girls* character
37 Margie Albright portrayer
38 Take another job
39 Mary Martin/ Robert Preston musical of '66
41 *Street Scene* playwright Elmer
43 "When Will ___ Loved"
44 "Music of My Heart" group
47 First grade homework
50 Auto grille protector
51 N.L. MVP of 1998
54 Start of an Austen title
55 Certain college members
57 "Java" performer
58 Bandleader Puente
60 Horror film sounds
65 Yankovic et al.
67 *The Sum of All Fears* author
69 Buenos ___
70 Basin or bore preceder
72 Ski lifts
73 Shroud city
74 Expert
75 Alliance once headed by Haig
76 Creative inspiration
77 Barbershop call
79 Ring out
83 Call ___ day
84 Start of the fifth century

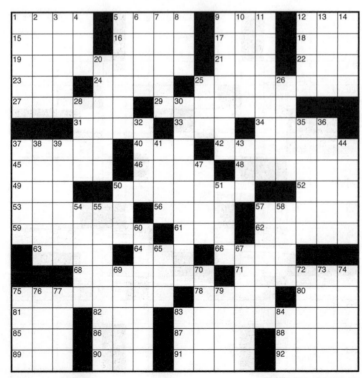

ANSWER, PAGE 60

Phobias

Others include triskaidekaphobia (the number 13), ailurophobia (cats), and arachibutyrophobia (peanut butter sticking to the roof of your mouth).

ACROSS

1 "The ___ of Amontillado"
5 1955 Kentucky Derby winner
10 Art sch. class
14 Suffix for suffer
15 Trap
16 Antitoxins
17 Monophobia
19 Mouthful of liquor
20 Bumbler
21 ___'acte
22 Feigns feelings
24 Dos Passos's *U.S.A.* is one
26 Antonín Dvořák, by birth
27 Blond shade
28 Combatant of 1899
29 "Big Blue"
32 Lewis's role in *The Nutty Professor*
35 *The Clan of the Cave Bear* author
37 Composer of the *Rocky* theme
39 Gephyrophobia
42 Baxter and Boleyn
43 "The Banana Boat Song"
44 Does not exist
45 ___ U.S. Patent Off.
46 FBI agents
48 Draft agcy.
50 Compound that expands when frozen
52 Toy dog
56 French novelist
58 Composer Schifrin
59 Little shaver
60 Gridiron unit
61 Panophobia
64 Designer Gernreich
65 *The Kiss* sculptor
66 Modicum
67 Alternatively
68 56-Across character
69 Alcyone or Algol

DOWN

1 Columbus contemporary
2 Keep ___ to the ground
3 Pulp magazine genre
4 Author Kesey
5 China's largest city
6 *Delta Wedding* author
7 Son of Venus
8 ATM ID
9 React to ragweed
10 Trade org.
11 Neophobia
12 Two-time Indy winner Luyendyk
13 Postscripts
18 Bygone GM autos
23 Tours "thanks"
25 Fall from grace
26 Cheese variety
28 Got started
30 Bingo call
31 *Gorillas in the ___*
32 '80s Chrysler category
33 Sea eagle
34 Sesquipedalo-phobia
36 Hypnotized
38 Horace, for one
40 Army NCOs
41 Former First Lady's first name
47 Cool Hand Luke was arrested for destroying them
49 Pigeonhole
51 WWII hero Murphy
52 Cheech's last name
53 British writer born in St. Louis
54 Word in many California city names
55 Candice's dad
56 Combustible heap
57 Actor Julia
58 Moon of Jupiter
62 Altar ritual
63 "___ Master's Voice"

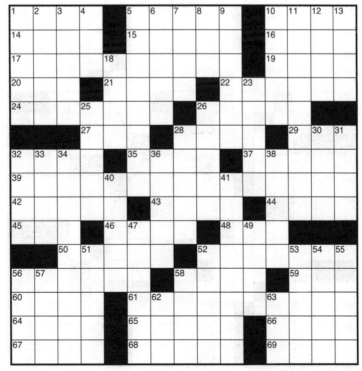

ANSWER, PAGE 62

Jelly Belly Flavors

Others include Toasted Marshmallow, Champagne Punch, Strawberry Cheesecake, and Chocolate Pudding.

ACROSS
1 Madison Square Garden, for one
6 Peruvian singer with a four-octave range
11 Elvis tune of '77
16 Photocopier supply
17 Smidgen
18 Discontinue
19 Jelly Belly flavor
21 Sean of *The Goonies*
22 Schwarzenegger film of '96
23 *Lifestyles of the Rich and Famous* host
25 Dict. entries
26 Compete in the Super G
27 Place for a boutonniere
29 Matt Groening's father's name, aptly
31 Caster starter
33 Zero
34 Jelly Belly flavor
37 PBS anchorman from '75 to '95
40 *The Sound of Music* tune
41 Juliet's surname
44 *Endeavour* launcher

46 Calif. airport
47 Elite group
48 1300 hours
50 Money-saving, in brand names
52 French diarist
53 Letters on some liquor
54 Justice Scalia
56 Calculator ancestor
59 Plot lines
61 Jelly Belly flavor
63 ACLU concern
64 S&L customer
68 Symbol for ohms
69 Plaster of Paris
71 "That's what *you* think!"
72 Stiller's girlfriend in *Meet the Parents*
74 Uses a microwave
76 Major ___ (some tarot cards)

78 *BUtterfield 8* author
80 Jelly Belly flavor
82 Biblical witch's home
83 German preposition
84 Hidden agenda
85 Best man's ritual
86 Final word
87 Rodeo animal

DOWN
1 Swear
2 *Diner* actor
3 Necessitate
4 Clears after taxes
5 Historian Durant
6 Former geopolitical initials
7 Hawaiian for "jumping flea"
8 Travel guide listing

9 Fictional terrier
10 Golfer Rodriguez
11 Former owner of Universal Studios
12 CBS sitcom that premiered in 2000
13 Jelly Belly flavor
14 *Clueless* catchphrase
15 Itches
20 Literature Nobelist of 1921
24 Harley competitor
28 Some beans or broncs
30 Alphabetic trio
32 Flightless birds
34 Show approval
35 Sultanate subject
36 *Six Crises* author
38 Space bar neighbor
39 Like Clouseau
41 Locks locale
42 Whodunit element

43 Jelly Belly flavor
45 Cleverness
49 Bordeaux bouquet
50 French season
51 ___ Nostra
53 Churchill trademark
55 Infiniti maker
57 Island group off Mozambique
58 Suffix for script
60 Euripides drama
62 Congressional group
65 Nickels and dimes
66 Menorah insert
67 "Casey at the Bat" writer
69 *My Life and Fortunes* autobiographer
70 Largest members of the dolphin family
72 Spenser or Spender
73 "Great Scott!"
75 Hawaiian coffee
77 Insincere talk
79 University department
81 ___ *y plata* (Montana's motto)

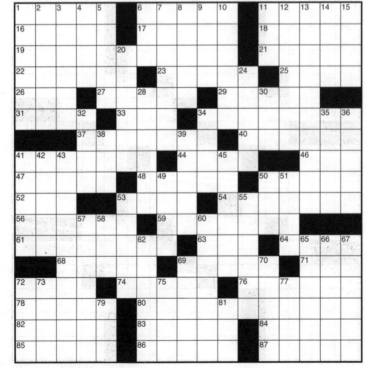

ANSWER, PAGE 56

Groucho Marx Roles

Others include Otis B. Driftwood (*A Night at the Opera*), Professor Quincy Adams Wagstaff (*Horse Feathers*), and J. Cheever Loophole (*At the Circus*).

ACROSS

1 Coloratura's pride
6 Disparaging remark
10 Hormel product
14 Chilean pianist
15 Jacob's twin
16 Muscle quality
17 Billy Goats Gruff adversary
18 Mad Libs fill-in
19 Lady Bird Johnson's middle name
20 Groucho, in *The Big Store*
23 Inventor Whitney
24 Internet service provider
25 "The Green Wave"
29 Dudevant's pen name
31 "___ Lazy River"
34 ___ end (done)
35 CAT creation
37 Reduces tension
39 Groucho, in *A Day at the Races*
42 Maine college town
43 *Yes ___* (Sammy Davis Jr. autobiography)
44 Like the White Rabbit
45 CPO's superior
46 It's taboo
48 "Old Rough and Ready"
50 Jamaican music
51 Erving's nickname
52 Groucho, in *Duck Soup*
59 Major Hoople exclamation
60 Scarlett's daughter in *Scarlett*
61 "___ Mio"
64 ___ breve
65 Offend the nose
66 *Get Yer ___ Out* (Rolling Stones album)
67 Clancy hero
68 Singer from Nigeria
69 Some convertible roofs

DOWN

1 Hedda Hopper trademark
2 Like "to be": Abbr.
3 Mature
4 Angel topper
5 Emcee of a record 23 TV game shows
6 Role portrayed by a dog named Higgins
7 Beginning
8 Gomez, in *Addams Family Values*
9 *Pilgrim's Progress* author
10 *60 Minutes* reporter
11 John Paul II, e.g.
12 Latin preposition
13 Ground grain
21 Discontinued Crayola color
22 Chief Anglo-Saxon god
25 *The Godfather Part II* setting
26 Road 180
27 Former African capital
28 Soon
29 Notorious '20s defendant
30 "The Times of Your Life" singer
31 Regular's order
32 Marinara alternative
33 Son of Jacob
36 *The Postman Always Rings Twice* author James
38 Well
40 Monty Hall booby prizes
41 ___ nous (confidentially)
47 *Rio Lobo* and *Rio Bravo*
49 Four-time Indy winner
50 Largest-area African country
51 Perry Mason's investigator
52 Aft
53 Like Cinderella's stepsisters
54 '40s First Dog
55 Dog bane
56 ___ *Three Lives*
57 Attorney-to-be's exam
58 Tom Smothers hobby
62 Baby seat
63 Half a figure eight

ANSWER, PAGE 58

World War II Code Names

Others include "Colonel Warden" (Winston Churchill),
"Glyptic" (Joseph Stalin), and "Workman" (Iwo Jima).

ACROSS

1 Renault, in *Casablanca*
6 Marilyn Monroe's dog
11 Obstetric procedure, for short
16 Shoelace tip
17 Onetime *TV Guide* reviewer
18 Home of Fordham
19 "Cactus"
21 Title car of a Harold Robbins novel
22 For example
23 Cell sections
24 House pest
25 H.S. class
26 Palm tree
28 "All the Things You ___"
29 Horrify
32 "Compost"
36 Judge in the news in '95
38 Proactive one
39 Part of the U.K.
40 Issue once debated by Gore and Perot
43 Yucca relative
47 "Duckpin"
52 "___ evil, hear ..."
53 Words on a Wonderland cake
54 Altar constellation

55 Off somewhere
58 Mary Tyler Moore role
61 "Dream"
66 *Frasier* dog
67 Winning streak
68 Thine: French
69 Health care professionals: Abbr.
70 007 adversary
73 Stanislavsky teaching
76 Taunting shout
79 Philosopher Kierkegaard
80 "Kilting"
82 "___ my case"
83 Open, as toothpaste
84 *A Bell for Adano* setting
85 *Jerusalem Delivered* poet

86 "Baloney!"
87 Haloid Company, today

DOWN

1 Alger hero's beginnings, so to speak
2 *Fuego* fighter
3 "Now ___ me down ..."
4 Captain Nemo's harpooner
5 Marvel Comics VIP
6 CCCXXV quadrupled
7 Shrinking Asian sea
8 New York's ___ (NYPD)
9 Song of Solomon follower

10 Continental divider: Abbr.
11 Singer Lane
12 He's "always on a steady course"
13 Passable
14 Cover
15 Photosynthesis product
20 Galoot
24 U2 leader
25 Chip shot path
27 Mercury or Saturn
29 Winter coasters
30 "___ talk?": Joan Rivers
31 Marty's pal, in *Marty*
32 Slightly
33 Complimentary
34 Slangy assent
35 Therefore
37 Part of IRS
41 Spanish relative

42 Prefix for physics
44 Golden Globe, for one
45 *Rigoletto* composer
46 Obliterate
48 Snarl
49 Allen Ginsberg poem
50 Mideast ruler
51 Computer monitor manufacturer
56 Melville monomaniac
57 Sun ___-sen
59 Guitarist at Woodstock
60 Program breaks
61 German toast
62 Author Welty
63 Guitarist Segovia
64 Gypsy language
65 *The Devil's Dictionary* author
69 Poppycock
71 Boxer Willard
72 In the know about
74 Airplane seat attachment
75 Overpromotion
76 Persian poet
77 Divine light
78 Mexican carving material
80 Droning sound
81 Salt Lake City collegian

ANSWER, PAGE 60

Monopoly Spaces

The most expensive property in the British version of Monopoly (corresponding to Boardwalk) is Mayfair.

ACROSS
1 Cultivator
5 Web addresses, for short
9 Piano part
14 Alternatively
15 In law, a minimum of three people is required for one
16 Game with a planchette
17 Space following Income Tax
20 It may acquit a defendant
21 Was of the opinion
22 Slips up
23 Periodic table abbr.
25 Canal device
27 '30s heavyweight boxing champ
30 Erstwhile gas brand
32 *Pocketful of Miracles* director
36 Garner of jazz
38 Presidential middle name
40 Around the 30th: Abbr.
41 Space following a Community Chest
44 Naval off.
45 Southeast Asian
46 What Dad called Kathy on *Father Knows Best*
47 Door closer
49 ___ B'rith
51 Horse height measure
52 Sister of Zeus
54 *Contact* org.
56 Indian royalty
59 D-Day beach
61 John Wayne, by birth
65 Space following St. Charles Place
68 South African leader
69 Spruce
70 Pesters
71 Attack
72 First word of "Send in the Clowns"
73 North Carolina county

DOWN
1 Bunch of bulls
2 Vegetable oil product
3 Biblical birthright barterer
4 Snoopy adversary
5 Samovar
6 American Civil Liberties Union concern
7 Folk stories
8 *First Blood* star
9 Patronage bestower
10 California's motto
11 "New Look" creator
12 Slightly open
13 The Four ___ ("Standing on the Corner" singers)
18 Mumbling cousin of sitcoms
19 Bachelor's last words
24 Cardiff citizens
26 LXXII tripled
27 Tropical nut
28 Gladiatorial venue
29 Physicist Mach
31 Yarn quantity
33 Numerical prefix
34 City on the Seine
35 Modify
37 Mythical river of forgetfulness
39 *The Great Dictator* Oscar nominee
42 1990 U.S. Open champ
43 Home of Gambela National Park
48 Dance step
50 Depth charge, in slang
53 Play with robots
55 Dickensian kid
56 Civil War side
57 Popular houseplant
58 James Dean, in *Giant*
60 Holes in one
62 Sandhurst studies
63 Egyptian cross
64 The Big Board: Abbr.
66 Sylvester, to Tweety
67 Giants' #4

ANSWER, PAGE 62

Symphony Nicknames

Others include "Winter Daydreams" (Tchaikovsky's #1),
"Choral" (Beethoven's #9), and "The Age of Anxiety" (Bernstein's #2).

ACROSS

1 "Thou ___ not then be false ...": Shakespeare
6 Statue of Liberty burden
11 Promoter's concerns
16 Martin song subject
17 Paul Tibbets's mother
18 "Fighting vainly the old ___": Cole Porter
19 Mendelssohn's #5
21 Actress Woodard
22 Adjective suffix
23 Pepsi rival
24 "There's no ___ in baseball!"
25 Emma Thompson ex
27 *Grinding It Out* autobiographer
29 Scot's refusal
30 Mia of *Ferris Bueller's Day Off*
31 Wash partner
34 Italian violinmaker
36 Discolor
38 Bullwinkle adversary
41 Fancy fabric
44 I ___ (Barbara Bush's license plate)
46 Pal

47 Pal
48 Shostakovich's #7
52 Clockmaker Terry
53 4,840 square yards
55 Peter Gunn's girlfriend
56 Medicine Nobelist of '58
58 Oldest city that's a U.S. state capital
61 *Escargots*
63 Didn't toss
64 '70s NATO commander
65 ___ of Maine (Crest competitor)
69 "___ on parle français"
71 Pastoral tale
73 Easter Island alias
75 Igneous rock sources

77 World's largest peninsula
80 Homophone for "heir"
81 Intelligence test developer
82 Bruckner's #7
84 Sister of Euterpe
85 Fay Vincent successor
86 Stairway post
87 Sorrow
88 Toboggans and luges
89 French school

DOWN

1 Indians that gave their name to a sea
2 Egyptian god of the universe
3 Extreme-sports slogan
4 Sign at a sellout

5 Earth: Latin
6 Arthur Chipping's occupation
7 Mindful of
8 Disturb
9 Dagger partner
10 Chinese dynasty
11 Early sports car
12 Just
13 Schubert's #8
14 ___ profit (make money)
15 Extended attack
20 Home run hero of '98
24 Robin Cook thriller
26 Agcy. established by Eisenhower
28 Purpose of a leave
32 Foul-smelling
33 Schumann's #3
35 *Tic ___ Dough*

37 $1,000,000, for short
39 Ship framework
40 Sand, to Chopin
41 Harvard degs.
42 *Jaws* boat
43 Haydn's #31
45 '60s rocket stage
49 Underprivileged
50 Mother of John Quincy
51 First st.
54 Greek letter
57 The Charleses' dog
59 Wiley Post, for one
60 G-men
62 Auto safety devices
66 Combination punch
67 Role for Toni in a 1994 Australian movie
68 *Fin de ___*
69 Fix firmly
70 Africa's largest city
72 Place for a button
74 "Band of Gold" singer Freda
76 "Take ___ your leader!"
78 Something to cast
79 H_2SO_4, e.g.
82 "The law is a ___": Dickens
83 Chest muscle, for short

ANSWER, PAGE 56

Saturday Night Live

Chevy Chase was a drummer for the rock group
Chameleon Church before becoming a regular on the program.

ACROSS

1 Two-band, perhaps
5 Santa's washday challenge
9 "Forever Your Girl" singer
14 Gaucho's device
15 Egyptian symbol of everlasting life
16 Warsaw money
17 British Airways' former name
18 Princess Amidala's daughter
19 Piano technician
20 Martin Short character
22 Demagnetize a videotape
23 "I've Got ___ in Kalamazoo"
24 Common abbreviation
26 Madison Avenue bunch
29 Jimi Hendrix wore one

31 Smooch
35 Long, in Hawaiian
36 Wile E. Coyote's supply company
38 *Purple Rain* artist
40 Catchphrase of the Church Lady
43 OAS member
44 Instance
45 ___-Star Pictures
46 Bucolic story
47 Pale
49 Start of a certain scale
51 Make a decision
52 Where Bette Midler grew up
54 Buck's adversary in *The Call of the Wild*
58 "Yeah, that's the ticket!" speaker
63 *I Love Lucy* executive producer

64 Evangelist Roberts
65 "Zip-___-Doo-Dah"
66 Actress friend of Valentino
67 Olympian queen
68 Symbol of Wales
69 Onrush
70 Ham's father
71 *The Producers* Tony winner

DOWN

1 Predecessor of Charo
2 "___ Indigo"
3 Stars and Bars, e.g.
4 Jones's *Carousel* costar Gordon ___
5 Frida portrayer in '02
6 Ogden Nash's "priest"
7 Steinbeck migrant

8 Henry Fonda's Oscar role
9 Stone calendar creator
10 Blinding flash
11 Spanish woman
12 Salt Lake City collegians
13 Orpheus's instrument
21 "Krazy Kat" mouse
25 Rival of Fleer and Donruss
26 Literally, "in another place"
27 Provided, as medication
28 Macho
30 Command to a canine
31 Paper Mate competitor
32 Karl Marx exhortation

33 Isadora Duncan's undoing
34 Bud of baseball
37 Word on every cover of *Mad* magazine
39 Iterate sonically
41 *Shop ___ You Drop*
42 Honshu farewell
48 Jill ___ of *Who's Minding the Store?*
50 Filmdom's Olive Oyl
51 *On the Town* sailor
53 Fifth word of the Koran
54 ___ *souci* (carefree)
55 Warm up, for short
56 Actress Swenson
57 *Alice in Wonderland* theft
59 Hydrox alternative
60 What a light bulb may symbolize
61 Archie or Jughead
62 Bert Lahr, in *The Wizard of Oz*

ANSWER, PAGE 58

Ad Slogans

Others include "Aim high" (U.S. Air Force),
"The dogs kids love to bite" (Armour), and "Just do it" (Nike).

ACROSS

1 Debbie Reynolds film role
6 *Jonny Quest* character of '60s TV
11 Pleasure boats
16 Battleground of 1836
17 Float ___ (get credit)
18 Dramatist Fugard
19 Like the *Ghostbusters* ghosts
20 "The company you keep"
22 "The best to you each morning"
24 Golf ball positions
25 Young Thomas Lincoln's nickname
26 Part of GPS
27 *The Ghost and ___ Muir*
28 Edson Arantes do Nascimento
29 Turtles and terriers
30 Ill-fated Heyerdahl craft
31 Whitney's invention
32 Half of CD
34 Bambi, for one
37 Golda's greeting
40 Orange Bowl home
43 Fusses
44 *The Music Man* hero
45 "___ Little Teapot"
47 Downcast
48 Alphabet run
49 "Just slightly ahead of our time"
51 Tetra- minus one
52 Peanut butter jar cover
53 Paramedic: Abbr.
54 Coll. hotshot
55 Ad award
56 *Answered Prayers* author
58 Handball variation
60 Shipped out
61 Beatles' meter maid
63 Coffee brewer
64 Alias: Abbr.
66 Talks too much
68 Four Seasons tune of '64
70 Elly May's dad
71 ___ Tafari (Haile Selassie)
74 Part of ETA
75 "It Must Be Him" singer Vikki
76 "When you care enough to send the very best"
78 "Be chewsy"
81 The vowels
82 Gerald Ford's birthplace
83 Conductor Koussevitsky
84 Kind of congestion
85 U-Haul competitor
86 Joyce Kilmer poem
87 Growl

DOWN

1 Things to do
2 Long's successor on *Cheers*
3 Ships out
4 CCCV × X
5 Cello fellow
6 "Thereby ___ a tale"
7 Pub servings
8 First editor of *The Wall Street Journal*
9 Car-collecting TV host
10 One way to fry
11 Asian bovines
12 Part of NATO
13 "Buy 'em by the sack"
14 Lite, on labels
15 Gravity-powered vehicles
21 '50s sitcom mom
23 *The Brethren* author
28 "Nothing says lovin' like something from the oven"
29 Greek letter
30 BP takers
31 Type of apple
33 Type of Apple
34 Bedford ___ (*It's a Wonderful Life* setting)
35 Word on a ticket
36 "Helps build strong bodies 12 ways"
38 Heloise offerings
39 Mythical king of Crete
41 Sausalito's county
42 Dostoyevsky title character
46 Biblical archangel
49 Astor commodity
50 Mideast sultanate
55 Letters on some Civil War belt buckles
57 ___ *for Evidence* (Grafton book)
59 It's .069 inches thick
62 Wise ___ owl
65 Canadian-born singer
66 *Queen of Outer Space* star
67 "You ___ Sunshine" (Louisiana state song)
69 Illegal oligopoly
70 Caan or Cagney
71 Former Russian First Lady
72 Clamorous
73 Jolly Roger symbol
75 Scorch
76 More than big
77 ___ Joe Greene
79 *Evita* character
80 ETS test

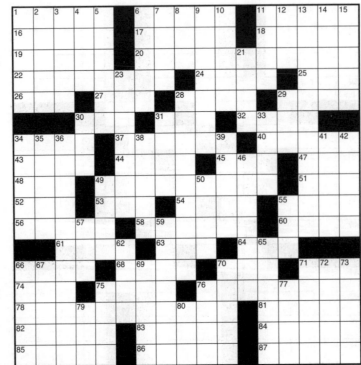

ANSWER, PAGE 60

James Bond Theme Singers

Others include Tom Jones (*Thunderball*),
Sheena Easton (*For Your Eyes Only*), and Madonna (*Die Another Day*).

ACROSS

1 Barney Rubble's voice
6 Caffeine-laden cola
10 Fractions of watts
14 One of Snoopy's brothers
15 World's bestselling cookie
16 Lean
17 Amtrak train
18 Test record
19 Not ___ many words
20 *The Spy Who Loved Me*
22 1982 Robin Williams role
23 Be obligated to
24 Prime time for Dracula
26 Fictional sleuth Lupin
30 Spoon handle
31 Cecile portrayer in *Dangerous Liaisons*
34 *Notes on a Cowardly Lion* subject
35 "If ___ I Would Leave You"
37 Tori's father
39 *Hansel and Gretel* appliance
40 Martinique volcano
42 Troop group
43 Crane relative
45 Financial aid criterion
46 Architect Saarinen
47 "___ port in a storm"
48 Porter relatives
50 Potsie Weber's real first name
52 South American capital
54 Kept a low profile
55 Bars to scan: Abbr.
57 *A View to a Kill*
63 Instrument not heard in *Duck Soup*
64 Monopoly card
65 Be penitent
66 One of the reeds
67 Reese Witherspoon, in *Legally Blonde*
68 Comedian who was once a rabbi
69 Kate Hudson's mom
70 Sunbeams
71 Alan Ladd film

DOWN

1 Bric-a-___
2 "Livin' La Vida ___"
3 State with conviction
4 Dudley Do-Right's girlfriend
5 Implement made of wax
6 Clarice portrayer before Julianne
7 With 59-Down, the Osmonds' hometown
8 Trini Lopez tune
9 Canada's $2 coin
10 Christian adversary
11 *GoldenEye*
12 Billy Joel concert site of '87
13 Organ part
21 Bert, in *Mary Poppins*
25 ABC show, initially
26 Last word on *Hawaii Five-O*
27 Poe bird
28 *Tomorrow Never Dies*
29 Professor Rubik
30 French Open champ, 1990–92
32 Wavelike silk design
33 Muriel spokesperson after Edie Adams, Susan ___
36 Country named for a city in Italy
38 Character actor Mischa
41 Duke Snider's real first name
44 Carpet feature
49 What Brits call a stocking run
51 Hull House founder
53 City on the Roaring Fork River
54 Mythical underworld
55 "Yipes!"
56 Sunblock chemical
58 Hinge (on)
59 See 7-Down
60 Parks of fame
61 Soon, in poems
62 Hawaiian goose

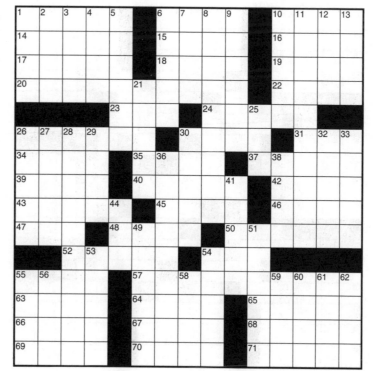

ANSWER, PAGE 62

Magic 8-Ball Messages

Others include "Better not tell you now,"
"Concentrate and ask again," and "Very doubtful."

ACROSS

1 South African statesman
6 *Chariots of Fire* star
11 Samuel L. Jackson role of '00
16 Hawaiian veranda
17 Grounds crews' roll-outs
18 1932 Winter Olympics star
19 Magic 8-Ball message
21 Golf pro's coup
22 "Here and there," in bibliographies
23 Miller of *On the Town*
24 *A Place for My Stuff* comedian
25 Ticklish Muppet
27 Visit
29 Mariner's septet
30 Explorer org.
33 Magic 8-Ball message
36 "No ifs, ___, or buts!"
38 Randy's skating partner
39 President at the Bicentennial
40 Leave locale for Hawkeye
42 Alf Landon's home: Abbr.
44 Verdi opera
49 Magic 8-Ball message
53 Conductor Toscanini
54 XVII × VI

55 *It Happened One Night* Oscar winner
56 *Long Day's Journey ___ Night*
59 Washington State's Sea-___ Airport
61 Vincent Lopez's theme song
62 Magic 8-Ball message
68 "Losing My Religion" rock group
69 Nabisco brand
70 ___ admiral
71 Walked on
73 Lack of practice
75 ___ Paulo
77 One of the Fates
81 "The Dapper Don"
82 Magic 8-Ball message

84 Scarlett O'Hara's mother
85 Dishwasher cycle
86 Untamed
87 Orchestra section
88 Part of NEA
89 One of the Muses

DOWN

1 Gaffe
2 ___ Hari
3 *Les États-___*
4 Cup: French
5 Vito Corleone's birthplace
6 Middle: Abbr.
7 Pro ___ (proportionally)
8 Syracuse University color
9 *The $64,000 Challenge*, for one
10 Bank acct. datum

11 Former National League park
12 Pulitzer rival
13 *Sense and Sensibility* director
14 Of child-parent relations
15 Wee
20 Actor M. ___ Walsh
24 *The Great Santini* author
26 Japanese city
28 *Familia* member
30 Iraq's only port
31 Villainous look
32 Emulate Daddy Warbucks
34 *Being John Malkovich* star
35 Luggage identifier
37 Shipmate of Chekov

41 Poetic domain of 89-Across
43 10001: Abbr.
45 First governor of Alaska
46 It brings out the child in you
47 De Gaulle's birthplace
48 Wee hour
50 Balzac's first name
51 Onetime Belgrade bigwig
52 Cheerful
57 When *Texaco Star Theater* was on: Abbr.
58 Olympic Airways founder
60 *The Odyssey* sorceress
62 '66 World Series player
63 '66 World Series player
64 Get comfy
65 Talked up
66 Stationmaster's concern
67 *Fiddler on the Roof* tune
72 Grandparent, often
74 Deadly septet
76 ___ buco
78 Supermodel Banks
79 Miami team
80 Birthplace of 18-Across
82 Coach Parseghian
83 Common Mkt.

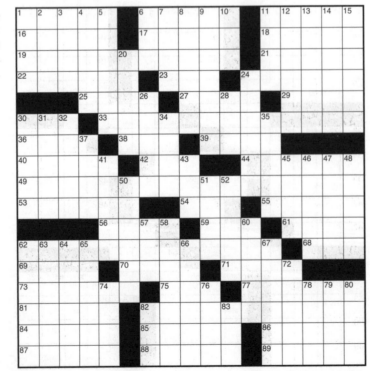

ANSWER, PAGE 57

Winston Churchill

The other books in Churchill's *Second World War* series are *The Gathering Storm*, *The Grand Alliance*, *The Hinge of Fate*, *Closing the Ring*, and *Triumph and Tragedy*.

ACROSS
1 Backyard building
5 Moisten, as a turkey
10 Suzanne's pet pig on *Designing Women*
14 Divine light
15 Intermission follower
16 Johnson of *Laugh-In*
17 "Back in the ___" (Beatles tune)
18 Pretend
19 Henri's head
20 One of Churchill's *Second World War* books
23 Geoffrey Rush's Oscar film
24 "___ Skylark" (Shelley ode)
25 Headline word of September 1974
28 With 42-Across, Churchill's middle names

32 Notions
33 Neckwear for Mr. T
35 Outback hopper
36 *Rose Marie* star
37 Rose protector
38 ___ the Clouds Roll By (Jerome Kern biopic)
39 ___ Lopez chess opening
40 Mideast patriarch
41 Loser
42 See 28-Across
44 Grant victory of 1862
45 Lout
46 Public-service cable network
48 The U.S. made Churchill one in '63
55 Earldom of 61-Across

56 "Far, a long, long way ___"
57 She followed Jesse Helms
58 Actress Kudrow
59 With 52-Down, Dreyfus defender
60 Astronaut Shepard
61 Churchill successor as prime minister
62 "She ___ seashells ..."
63 Buttermilk's rider

DOWN
1 Close up
2 Miscellany
3 Ultimatum ending
4 "Que Sera, Sera" singer
5 Explorer of arctic North America
6 ___ the hole (secret weapon)

7 Popular children's author
8 Buster Brown's dog
9 Physics Nobelist of 1921
10 *Guys and Dolls* character
11 Black-and-white treat
12 Part of a Julius Caesar quote
13 Rude look
21 Greek letters
22 Roger Rabbit, for one
25 ___ *Plowman* (English poem)
26 Make sense
27 Change colors again
28 Carefree adventure
29 Disney's Little Mermaid

30 Loggers' contest
31 Sylvester's opponent in *Rocky IV*
33 "The Way of Love" singer
34 ___ polloi
37 Atropos and her sisters
38 Columbus landfall of 1498
40 Lasting impression
41 French feline
43 Earhart's navigator Fred
44 Porcupine quills
46 "Apostle of the Slavs"
47 Boat that is oared
48 *Gilligan's Island* star Alan
49 *Ars Amatoria* poet
50 Snoop (around)
51 City served by Da Vinci Airport
52 See 59-Across
53 Airline to Israel
54 Oahu goose

ANSWER, PAGE 59

Boy Scout Merit Badges

Others include Auto Mechanics, Oceanography, and Stamp Collecting.

ACROSS

1 Syrup flavor
6 Cashew tree relative
11 Old radio's Major ___
16 Annoyed
17 *All My Children* character
18 Cheer for a diva
19 Boy Scout merit badge
21 *Gremlins* actress Phoebe ___
22 Comparative suffix
23 Part of NRA or NRA
24 Sri Lanka export
26 Hawaiian honker
27 John Havlicek's team
29 Make-___ Foundation
31 Turn signal directions: Abbr.
32 *Foucault's Pendulum* author
33 British preppies
35 Agenda, for short
38 Rom. ___
40 *Star Trek: First Contact* director Jonathan
43 Animation frames
44 Makes airtight, in a way
47 Jefferson, for one
48 *The Facts of Life* actress
49 Boy Scout merit badge
51 "Am ___ understand ..."
52 Bring on
54 Small garment size
55 Was sure of
56 Amelia Earhart's publisher husband

58 "___ Mommy Kissing Santa Claus"
59 Curved molding
60 Lab work
63 Publisher's nickname
65 Key letter
67 Grain holders
68 Daryl Hannah, in *Splash*
72 Roll partner
74 Sigma preceder
75 Mata ___
76 "Xanadu" group
77 Thomas of basketball
79 Boy Scout merit badge
82 Met competitor
83 Take another shot
84 Actor Davis
85 Big name in hot dogs

86 A, B, and O
87 They're often counted

DOWN

1 Penn's specialty
2 Up ___ (trapped)
3 30th wedding anniversary gift
4 Santa Claus perch
5 Racial
6 Religious offshoots
7 Russian river
8 Russian for "peace"
9 When Juliet says "What's in a name?"
10 Compound in milk from which cheese is made
11 *Fawlty Towers* network
12 Port of Algeria

13 Boy Scout merit badge
14 One of five in a pentathlon
15 Return-mail conveniences: Abbr.
20 He developed the Mustang
25 What "quasi" means
28 Turner's namesakes
29 Boy Scout merit badge
30 "Game" starts with one
33 Piano piece
34 Scottish refusal
35 Temporary currency
36 Sandra's *Speed* costar

37 Boy Scout merit badge
39 *My Generation* company
41 Big name in makeup
42 Trapp Family Inn locale
45 Potato concoction
46 *Ramayana* character
49 *The Tin Drum* author
50 He recorded *The Button-Down Mind*
53 A, in Arles
55 Former U.N. leader Annan
57 Ingrid Bergman role of 1982
61 *The Green Hornet* theme player
62 *60 Minutes* commentator
64 Stock ticker inventor
65 Father of Cassandra
66 Daniel follower
68 *Miracle on 34th Street* store
69 *Horton Hears a Who* author
70 Any *Hit Parade* tune
71 "The Highwayman" poet
73 *New York Inquirer* publisher, in film
75 "You are ___"
78 Part of a Ralph Kramden laugh
80 "The racer's edge"
81 General on Chinese menus

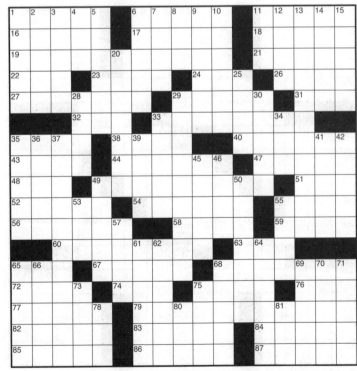

ANSWER, PAGE 61

Country Music Nicknames

Others include "The Brakeman" (Jimmie Rodgers),
"The Man in Black" (Johnny Cash), and "Bocephus" (Hank Williams Jr.).

ACROSS
1 Letter stroke
6 Dog with a blue-black tongue
10 Commit a football infraction
14 Rocket type
15 *I Owe Russia $1200* author
16 Swarm home
17 Motel alternative
18 Explorer Tasman
19 Send out
20 "The Tennessee Plowboy"
22 Muscle quality
23 "The Entertainer" is one
24 Smart-mouthed
25 State trooper, to a CBer
29 *My Fair Lady* setting
32 Nimoy's *Mission: Impossible* role
33 Mary Quant creation
37 Med. school course
38 New Hampshire's state flower
39 ___-Tass
40 Traditional drink at the Kentucky Derby
42 Plumber's tool
43 Disgusting, to a kid
44 *Return of the Native* setting
45 *Porgy and Bess* villain
48 Aircraft-registration agcy.
49 Brickyard event
50 "The Texas Troubadour"
57 Footnote abbr.
58 Uncultured sort
59 *Fiddler on the Roof* star
60 Rossini subject
61 Real estate abbreviation
62 Spandex brand
63 Pitching stats
64 Tractor-trailer
65 Sibilant sounds

DOWN
1 Kemo ___
2 "Heavens to Betsy!"
3 Pull apart
4 Nickname of a Harrison Ford character
5 "Johnny Angel" singer
6 1989 French Open champ
7 Rail rider
8 G.M. European subsidiary
9 Thalia Menninger portrayer in *The Many Loves of Dobie Gillis*
10 "Mr. Guitar"
11 Prom rentals
12 *Nothin' but Good Times Ahead* author
13 *Little Rascals* dog
21 *Rebel Without a Cause* director
24 Successor of CQD
25 Bulk e-mail
26 "The ___ Love" (Gershwin tune)
27 *The Plague* locale
28 "The Queen of Country Music"
29 Choreographer of Bernstein's *Mass*
30 Cereal mascot in a baker's hat
31 Presidential title: Abbr.
33 "Got ___?"
34 *Play ___ It Lays*
35 Hogarth subject
36 *The Lost World* terror
38 Jean-___ Godard
41 End of the 2nd qtr.
42 Alaska cruise starting point
44 *The Man Who Never ___*
45 Where Knossos is located
46 Standard and Poor's, e.g.
47 City near Gainesville
48 Manhattan Project VIP
50 Recedes
51 Was a passenger on
52 Comedian Crosby
53 Mattel merchandise
54 Product IDs
55 Dull one
56 *Gil ___* (Lesage novel)

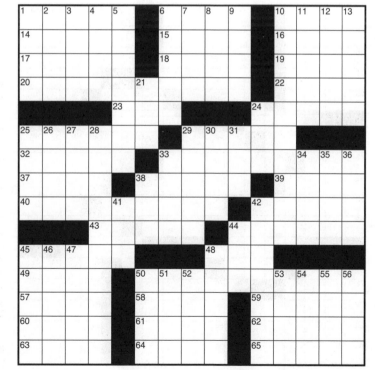

ANSWER, PAGE 63

Double Academy Award Winners

Others include Bette Davis (*Dangerous*, *Jezebel*), Jessica Lange (*Tootsie*, *Blue Sky*), and Spencer Tracy (*Captains Courageous*, *Boys Town*).

ACROSS

1 Fab Four flick
5 *Wall St. Lays* ___ (memorable *Variety* headline)
10 Designer whose real first name was Gabrielle
16 Av follower, in the Hebrew calendar
17 Counterculture guru
18 First product in the first TV commercial
19 It's about 17 million square miles
20 *Spartacus* and *Topkapi*
22 Optimistic
23 Perry White's job
24 Fake out, in ice hockey
25 Iditarod vehicle
26 Glenn's *Gilda* costar
27 "___ to Rio" (Peter Allen tune)
30 Painter Gerard ___ Borch
31 Show team spirit
33 *High Noon* theme singer
35 ___ *Shimbun* (Japanese newspaper)
37 *The French Connection* and *Unforgiven*
43 ASCAP rival
44 Attacked
46 Bring to naught
47 "___ Cassius has a lean and hungry look"

49 A French defensive barrier was named for him
51 Some drill instructors: Abbr.
52 Hi-fi
54 Songlike
56 "Vamoose!"
57 *Kramer vs. Kramer* and *Sophie's Choice*
59 Grand narratives
61 *The ___ of the Fisherman* (Morris West novel)
62 Dumas ___ (D'Artagnan creator)
63 RR stop
66 Verb suffix
67 Kiss partner
70 Gomer Pyle's gp.
73 Argentine uncles
75 C.S. Lewis land
77 Hoskins, in *Hook*
78 *Viva Zapata!* and *Lust for Life*
81 Pie-cooling place
82 Neighbor of Taurus
83 Lexicographer's concern
84 "Let ___ Me" (Everlys tune)
85 Its name changed after Russia joined it
86 Fancy neckwear
87 Captain of the *Pequod*

DOWN

1 Learns about
2 The sun, in Seville
3 *The Great Ziegfeld* and *The Good Earth*
4 Toy originally sold as a wallpaper cleaner
5 A&M Records cofounder Herb
6 "___ say more?"
7 "Weird Al" parody tune
8 *Grand Hotel* name
9 Greek sandwich
10 Paley's network
11 Home for Gilligan
12 "Put ___ on it!"
13 Work for nine
14 Call forth
15 Roy Emerson contemporary Rod
21 *David Copperfield* clerk
28 Christy Mathewson's team
29 First word of "The Raven"
32 Peanut product
33 *Of Mice and Men* character
34 Cardiology charts: Abbr.
35 Bottomless pit
36 Struck down
37 Angelina Jolie role
38 Mystery writers' awards
39 Bête ___
40 *The Prime of Miss Jean Brodie* and *California Suite*
41 *Toys in the ___*
42 Hornets' homes
45 Israeli novelist
48 WCTU members
50 "Alley ___"
53 Pre-college
55 Oxford specification
58 Microscopic
60 Frederick the Great's domain
62 Vulcan or Tralfamadore
63 "The Grand Old Man of Football"
64 Fork parts
65 Phrase of denial
67 Type of bridge
68 Early computer
69 Jargon
71 Peach ___
72 *Us* subject
74 Hood's knife
76 Water: Latin
79 Unspecified person
80 *Henry & June* character

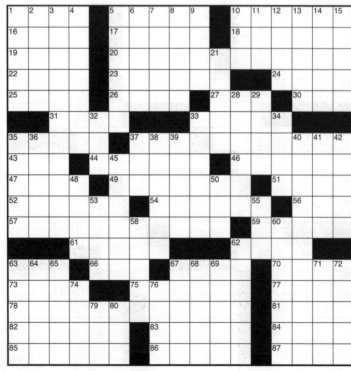

ANSWER, PAGE 57

U.S. Coin Mottoes

17-/62-Across appeared on
U.S. pennies in 1787.

ACROSS

1 Gun, as an engine
4 High point
8 *Buck Privates* star Bud
14 Gold: Spanish
15 Ancient Mideast kingdom
16 "___, My God, to Thee"
17 With 62-Across, first motto to appear on U.S. coins
19 Actor Fred who became a congressman
20 Overture follower
21 Potter rabbit
23 "___ for her eyes, with love-light shining"
24 Kurt Cobain's group
27 Falcons, on scoreboards
28 Same old thing
29 Muckraker Tarbell
30 Uses mucilage
32 Exercise rooms
33 Type of skiing
35 Habitual practice
38 Motto on current U.S. coins
42 Japanese immigrant
43 Boxing-related
45 Italian princely surname
48 Open to bribery
50 Dungeons & Dragons publisher
51 Top bond rating
52 Ending for system
54 Radio City Music Hall style
56 *77 Sunset Strip* character
57 Tycoon from Texarkana
59 Historical periods
60 Musical that introduced "Cheek to Cheek"
62 See 17-Across
65 Queen Elizabeth I epithet
66 Mesopotamia, today
67 I-80, for one
68 Turtle toon quartet
69 "I don't mind ___, except as meals": Odgen Nash
70 Conscription agcy.

DOWN

1 Where Transylvania is
2 *Life of Brian* star
3 *The Sound of Music* surname
4 Alcott character
5 Dove sound
6 '50s Kenyan revolutionary
7 Spain's longest river
8 "The King of ___" (comedian Richard Lewis)
9 Aviator Markham
10 Sound at a shearing
11 Stubborn
12 That yawning feeling
13 Secret get-togethers
18 Subsidiary: Abbr.
22 *Pari* ___ (fairly)
25 ___ Dei
26 Cards and Astros
31 Ragtime composer James Blake's nickname
32 DoD brass
34 Nastase of tennis
36 ___ as the eye can see
37 Culpability
39 "If ___ catch you ..."
40 Speakers
41 Has Arnold Schwarzenegger play Peter Pan, e.g.
44 Noughts-and-___ (tic-tac-toe, in Britain)
45 "What Comes Naturally" singer Sheena
46 Sudden enlightenment, in Zen
47 Elton John collaborator
49 Weekly science magazine
52 Bucky Beaver's toothpaste
53 Greek letters
55 Cub Scout group
58 Drama award
61 Uris novel, with *The*
63 Gal of song
64 Measures of brightness

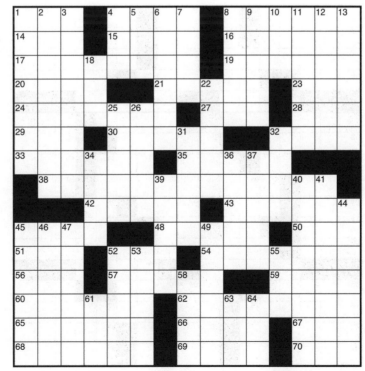

ANSWER, PAGE 59

Stephen King

King used the pen name Richard Bachman for seven novels,
including *The Running Man* and *Thinner*.

ACROSS

1 Longest human bone
6 Leif's dad
10 Miscues
16 Whirlpool competitor
17 "To Sir With Love" singer
18 Parliamentary procedure expert
19 Colorado setting of *Misery*
21 Senator from Hawaii
22 Chic Johnson's partner
23 Father's Day gift
25 Center for Auto Safety founder
26 Lobbying gp.
28 Where to find the Fool and the Hermit
30 Setting of *The Shining*
35 "Carry moonbeams home in a ___"
38 *Challenger* astronaut Judith
39 Unforgiving
40 In the style of
41 Mary Kay rival
42 Office-computer acronym
43 Occupational suffix
45 Nada
46 Health club
47 Film based on a King novella
50 Prepare leftovers, perhaps
51 Lunar New Year

52 Norse god of strife
53 Boy of song
54 Portrait on a $10,000 bill
56 Poetic preposition
57 Scottish sport pole
59 *Dirty Harry* director Don
60 Radiator sound
61 King's publishing company
63 Julia Roberts's middle name
64 Privation
65 Chicago Seven colleague
68 Necessitate
71 102, in old Rome
74 Trumpeter from New Orleans
76 Maine setting of *Cujo*
79 Quantum theory originator

80 Socks
81 Melville novel
82 Small band
83 Cornerstone abbr.
84 Fronton device

DOWN

1 Burkina ___
2 Pianist Gilels
3 "Looks Like We ___ It" (Manilow tune)
4 French article
5 Like sushi
6 Climate-affecting current
7 Ill-mannered
8 "___ a Song Go Out of My Heart"
9 Museum VIP
10 Datebook abbr.
11 Former world leader with a palindromic name

12 WWII sub
13 Jack Benny and Fred Allen had one
14 Impressionist David who specialized in Nixon
15 Ending for joke or trick
20 "No problem!"
24 Type of marble
26 "Rule, Britannia" composer
27 Most shrewd
29 Adjust a dress
30 Brother of Electra
31 Evening service
32 Probate lawyer's concern
33 *Star Trek II* villain
34 Telephone part
35 The F. Scott Fitzgerald era

36 Rap sheet listing
37 Mountaineer's maneuvers
42 Actress Day in '40s movies
44 Child offering
48 Prominent lunar crater named after an astronomer
49 Gore Vidal historical novel
55 Thundering ___ (Woody Herman's orchestra)
58 Vivien's role in *A Streetcar Named Desire*
59 Common sense
61 14th president
62 Delta alternative
63 Fire starter
65 ___ at Sea (Laurel and Hardy film)
66 French pronoun
67 Cries of discovery
69 Marshal McCloud's hometown
70 Aide: Abbr.
71 Toody and Muldoon, in *Car 54, Where Are You?*
72 Tracy Marrow's stage name
73 Home furnishings giant
75 Box office buy: Abbr.
77 List shortener
78 Ingredient in an Old Fashioned

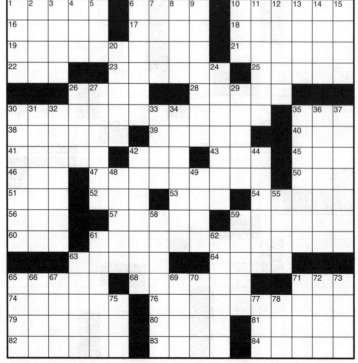

ANSWER, PAGE 61

Summer Olympics Sites

Others include Amsterdam (1928),
Helsinki (1952), and Beijing (2008).

ACROSS
1 Metallic fabric
5 Queen Elizabeth's dressmaker
10 Skeptical response
14 Inventor Sikorsky
15 *The 39 Steps* star
16 *The Persistence of Memory* artist
17 1968
19 *If ___ the Zoo* (Seuss book)
20 *West Side Story* character
21 Recipe direction
22 Summit
23 Speaker system
25 Frequent George Shearing partner
27 Kornelia ___ (first woman to win four gold medals in one Olympics)
30 Caught red-handed

33 One of television's first successful sitcoms
36 Altar exchanges
38 Winter forecast
39 "___ You Lonesome Tonight?"
40 1920
42 Eleanor Roosevelt, ___ Roosevelt
43 Devours, with "down"
45 Literally, "I forbid"
46 Talk back to
47 Scotch cocktail
49 Neighbor of Mary Richards
51 *CHiPs* actress Randi
53 Agent 99 portrayer
57 Mythical man-goat
59 Boxer Firpo

62 Daughter of Tantalus
63 Lie in the weeds
64 1984
66 River of Italy
67 Last Greek letter
68 Music marking
69 Singer at Woodstock
70 *Bullets Over Broadway* Oscar winner
71 January 13th

DOWN
1 Succotash ingredients
2 Catalyst
3 Nehi competitor
4 Nation on the Red Sea
5 Fuss
6 Summer shoes, for short

7 "What's ___ for me?"
8 Yankovic tune
9 *Sophie's Choice* author
10 1950s heavyweight boxing champ of Uganda
11 1992
12 *Support Your Local Sheriff* actor Jack
13 Pitchfork part
18 Pulitzer-winning columnist Herb
24 Valhalla VIP
26 Gravelly voice
28 Ron Howard film of '99
29 Crew team member
31 Fleecing candidates
32 M&M's colorings
33 Bryn ___
34 Ending for buck

35 1956
37 *Murder, She Wrote* doc
40 "Dilbert" employee
41 Skylight site
44 Voice of Miss Piggy
46 F. Murray Abraham Oscar role
48 Sea that separates Korea and China
50 Long March participant
52 Finland, in Finland
54 Parceled (out)
55 Like Jabba the Hutt
56 Snug spots
57 Bodybuilder's bane
58 New Age glow
60 "Nothing but blue skies do ___"
61 Loses tautness
65 Lithographer Currier's nickname

ANSWER, PAGE 63

Mottoes

Others include "All the News That Fits" (Rolling Stone), "Fidelity, Bravery, Integrity" (F.B.I.), and "Service Above Self" (Rotary International).

ACROSS

1 Oath taker's response
4 *The Merchant of Venice* character
10 *Inherit the Wind* inspiration
16 Sound stage
17 Inuit relatives
18 City south of Seattle
19 *Wheel of Fortune* purchase
20 "Blood and Fire"
22 Formal dances
24 *Robots and Empire* author
25 Prof.'s aides
26 High-fashion mag
27 Airline abbreviation
29 Melodies of India
31 "Liberty, Intelligence, Our Nation's Safety"
34 F alias
38 Oscar ___ Renta
39 Part of SALT
42 "What ___ mind reader?"
43 Pharaoh headdress symbol
46 Yellow dog, for short
47 Swee' ___
48 Hinder
49 "He best serves himself who serves others"
53 P&G products
54 Pronoun for Miss Piggy

55 "Penguin" of baseball
56 General of Chinese cuisine
57 Double-play pair
58 Charlie Brown exclamation
59 "How clumsy of me!"
61 Shrimp style
63 *Vince aut morire* (conquer or die)
68 Center
71 "Open 9 ___ 5"
72 Clytemnestra's mother
73 "___ the fields we go ..."
76 Foe of U.N.C.L.E.
78 Surrealist works
79 *Ich dien* (I serve)
83 Extra NHL periods
84 Inventor Otis

85 "The 1½ Calorie Breath Mint"
86 One ___ customer
87 Iterated
88 Brain power
89 Play about Capote

DOWN

1 Señora Perón after Evita
2 Mount McKinley's other name
3 Opera that premiered at La Scala
4 Brenner or Khyber
5 Slangy suffix
6 Fam. member
7 Country that licenses its .tv Internet suffix
8 "Take ___ a compliment!"
9 Out of bed

10 "Some More of Samoa" trio
11 Tent material
12 South American tuber
13 Wine that originated in Iberia
14 Madame Bovary
15 Simon ___
21 "___ Yankee Doodle dandy ..."
23 Provide at interest
27 Bruin
28 "Mountain Music" group
30 Sea World whale
32 Tennis star from Yugoslavia
33 One of the sacraments
35 Scope
36 Teheran money
37 *Saturday Night Live* announcer

40 '20s auto
41 Physics Nobelist of 1909
43 Trade org.
44 Use steel wool on
45 Yammer
48 *The Ten Commandments* setting
50 Derby town
51 Trig. function
52 Asian capital
58 Mark Twain, for one
60 *Sisters* name
62 Chinese nut
64 Cornell's home
65 John McGraw protégé
66 Helen Gurley Brown, e.g.
67 Type of golf bet
69 Seatless situation: Abbr.
70 Massachusetts university
73 Abbreviation near 0
74 ___ Stanley Gardner
75 *How the Other Half Lives* author
77 Emulate Weissmuller
78 Mil. medals
80 Cryptologic Museum sponsor: Abbr.
81 Env. contents
82 Grandma's exhortation

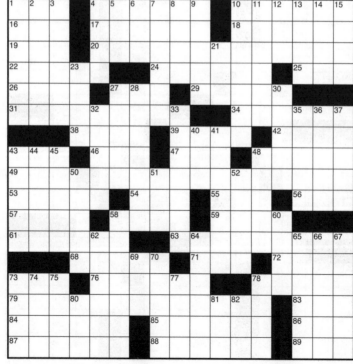

ANSWER, PAGE 57

Stars' Film Production Companies

Others include Overbrook Entertainment (Will Smith),
Fountainbridge Films (Sean Connery), and Prufrock Pictures (Meg Ryan).

ACROSS

1 Kodak competitor
5 Three-stripers: Abbr.
9 ___ facto
13 Youngest Greek god
14 Senior lobby
15 Physicist Bohr
17 Goat Cay Productions
20 Org. once headed by Lewis Hershey
21 Popular successes
22 Colleague of Blake, Stone, and Weaver
23 *Grand Theft* ___ (first film directed by Ron Howard)
24 Soprano colleague
25 Barwood Films
32 Actor Milo
33 Tabula ___
34 Southeast Asian
35 Actor ___ Patrick Harris

36 Addis ___
38 *Waiting for Godot* character, for short
39 Martial arts level
40 Laser, for one
41 Dwarf complement
42 Amblin Entertainment
46 Father of Phobos
47 The Munsters' pet
48 Designer Versace
51 Kaput
52 British equivalent of S.S.
55 Shamley Productions
58 Endorses
59 Sundance Film Festival locale
60 Roentgen discovery
61 British composer
62 That lady's
63 *Daily Planet* reporter

DOWN

1 Admit everything, with "up"
2 *Battle Cry* author
3 Runs for health
4 It means "equal"
5 Tokyo airport
6 Byron's *Don Juan* has 17 of them
7 Galena and bauxite
8 Matt Helm, e.g.
9 Subject of Newton's First Law of Motion
10 Yamaha products
11 Golfer Ballesteros

12 Words a toreador adores
16 Gown renters: Abbr.
18 *Star Trek* bridge officer
19 Peace Nobelist of '83
23 Biblical shepherd
24 Part of UAR
25 Only seven-time baseball MVP
26 Have ___ (rest)
27 German wine valley
28 Chaplin persona
29 Survival film set in the Andes
30 Green Party VIP
31 Up to
36 Trojan War epic

37 Stringed instrument
38 What red ink represents
40 ___ Alps (Swiss range)
41 Exemplar of laziness
43 Rembrandt's last name
44 Beatty/Hoffman film
45 Pliocene and Eocene
48 Federal auditing agcy.
49 Actress Chase
50 Worship from ___
51 Hardhat's workplace
52 Circle dance
53 Shoe merchant Thom
54 Donovan's daughter Ione
56 "What was that?"
57 XXXV × IV

ANSWER, PAGE 59

Ticker-Tape Parade
Multiple Honorees

Others include Charles de Gaulle (1945, 1960),
Dwight Eisenhower (1945, 1960), and Haile Selassie (1954, 1963).

ACROSS

1 Master, in Madras
6 Whodunit plot element
11 Brother of J.R. Ewing
16 It was discovered by Clyde Tombaugh in 1930
17 Try to buy at auction
18 *Rocky* victor
19 Aviator (1926, 1927, 1930)
21 Gary Cooper role
22 Fannie ___
23 Maleficent's pet raven in *Sleeping Beauty*
24 Summer sign
25 Author Kosinski
26 Start of the seventh century
28 Strength: Latin
31 Dole, in 1996
34 Aviator (1931, 1933)
37 Its acad. is in New London
38 New York college
39 Fictional falcon's origin
40 "Hold on a ___!"
41 Home-based business of a sort
44 Type of tooth
46 Aviator (1928, 1932)
49 Poker ploy
51 Football team at 38-Across
52 Afore
55 Chemical needed for muscle contraction
56 ___ Bay, Oregon
58 Jethro Bodine portrayer

59 Astronaut (1962, 1998)
61 Escamillo, in *Carmen*
64 "___ Bonds Today?" (WWII song)
65 Linguistic suffix
66 *Oliver Twist* villain
67 Thunderbolt sound in "B.C."
69 20th-century coloratura
71 To's opposite
74 Pâté ingredient
77 Baseball team (1962, 1969, 1986)
79 "I'm Just Wild About Harry" composer
80 "Rings ___ fingers ..."

81 Art store purchase
82 *Cannonball Express* engineer
83 *The NeverEnding ___*
84 *Rinaldo* poet

DOWN

1 GI entree
2 He originated the role of Sky Masterson
3 Jessica's husband
4 "Lord, is ___?"
5 Condensed milk inventor
6 On fire
7 "Scooter" ___ (name in 2007 news)
8 Pastoral poem

9 Composer who was also a chemist
10 Where the Wabash flows: Abbr.
11 Alphabetic quartet
12 Sweet sandwich
13 Opie Taylor's great-aunt
14 Four-poster
15 Golf scorecard abbr.
20 Suffix for million
24 Hammarskjöld predecessor
25 Joyful dance
27 Actress Danes
28 Act enforced by the 18th Amendment
29 Ratio phrase
30 Castor or Pollux
31 Greek letters
32 Sugary suffix

33 Snerd's colleague
34 Lake popularized by Keillor
35 Places to learn to swim
36 Matching set
38 Rhoda's mother
41 *The Unbearable Lightness of ___*
42 Roker et al.
43 Reunion attendees
45 66-Down's gp.
47 Ma Kettle portrayer Marjorie
48 ___ in apple
49 Prince of India
50 Nobel Prize category: Abbr.
53 Model T contemporary
54 Make a mess of things
57 Words on a penny
58 Secret rival
60 Diminutive suffix
61 *Le Morte d'Arthur* writer
62 Lab culture
63 Second word of an Ella Fitzgerald tune
66 Philadelphia athlete
67 Cowardly Lion's alter ego
68 Mine rocks
70 *Horton Hears ___!* (Seuss book)
71 Actor Parker
72 Motorist's alternatives: Abbr.
73 Christiania, today
74 Robert Caro biography subject
75 U.N. workers' agency
76 Lee ___ Cleef
77 Turndowns
78 Lamb's sound

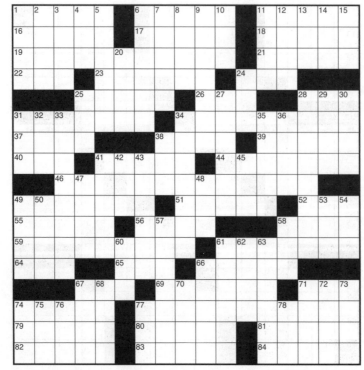

ANSWER, PAGE 61

Fast Food

Each McDonald's regular hamburger has a
precooked weight of 1.6 ounces.

ACROSS

1 Form of water
6 XXIV × VIII
11 Ted Baxter's employer
14 Madonna film role
15 Put up ___ (act up)
16 "Bali ___"
17 Byways
18 ___ Bornes (card game)
19 Coveted NCAA position
20 She shouted "Where's the beef?" for Wendy's
22 Permanent marker
23 French roast
24 Valuable rock
25 Ooze
27 *Cat ___ Hot Tin Roof*
28 Let gravity move you
30 *Coming of Age in Samoa* author
33 Lead balloon
34 British spy novelist
37 Gilda Radner character Emily
41 Braque and Picasso

42 Dr. John McIntyre's nickname
43 Stylist's substance
44 Amish, for example
45 Brother of Flopsy and Mopsy
48 1948 song "Once in Love With ___"
51 Exclamation of dread
54 Allegro ___ brio
55 Plumlike fruit
56 Its name is an abbreviation for "Committee for State Security"
58 They average 178 on a Big Mac bun
61 "Just the Way You ___" (Billy Joel tune)
62 Frighten

63 Magic spells
64 Not even one
65 Sammy the Bull ratted on him
66 *Dirty Dancing* director Ardolino
67 Blow up: Abbr.
68 Friend of Elizabeth I
69 Adjutants: Abbr.

DOWN

1 George de Mestral's invention
2 Arthurian paradise
3 Mexican party purchase
4 Cheri of *Saturday Night Live*
5 Tabula ___ (clean slate)
6 Mathew Brady's meal ticket

7 Mulder/Scully investigations
8 Select
9 NHL team, familiarly
10 Grenoble's river
11 They cost 37¢ when first introduced in 1957
12 Maureen O'Sullivan role opposite Johnny Weissmuller
13 Attitude
21 Illustration on some skirts
26 Spam, for example
28 *I Spy* star
29 Close attention: Abbr.
31 Uffizi display
32 ___ Plaines, Illinois

33 One of the dimensions
35 University of Oregon home
36 Radio-active driver
37 Recent USMA graduates
38 Make angry
39 Chain that used a Chihuahua as its mascot
40 Dada painter
46 Two-player card game
47 TM-Bar Ranch cowboy
48 Krystle Carrington nemesis
49 One of 15,456,868 built from 1908 to 1927
50 Thumbs-up votes
52 Inedible orange
53 Copters
55 Looks to be
56 The "Boop-Oop-a-Doop Girl" Helen
57 Cheshire Cat expression
59 Coll. admission criteria
60 Ballpark from 1964 to 2008

P.D.Q. Bach Works

Others include *"Unbegun" Symphony*,
"O Little Town of Hackensack," and *Rounds for Squares*.

ACROSS

1 Tubby, for one
5 Sabrina's pet cat
10 Like Steve Austin
16 Menace in a '58 sci-fi film
17 Garlic portion
18 Garner of jazz
19 P.D.Q. Bach work
21 *The Chronicles of ___* (C.S. Lewis magnum opus)
22 Was missing
23 Golf hole edge
25 Emulate eagles
26 City near Düsseldorf
27 Toscanini was once its musical director
31 Bilko, for one: Abbr.
32 Base runner's achievement
34 Harlem music hall
36 Stat. measure
39 "The Man Without a Country" exile
41 Online newsgroup system
44 *Royal ___ Musick* (P.D.Q. Bach work)
47 Bric-a-brac stand
48 Do penance
49 Mind another's business
51 Make a dance-floor move
52 Having a tail
54 P.D.Q. Bach work
56 Mortise partners
57 Lachrymose
58 Curved letter
59 Marvelous
61 *Brigadoon* composer
64 Not "agin"
66 Oil changer's need
68 *Watership Down* author
72 Fission candidate
74 BB propellant
75 1850s war zone
76 *___ Is My Life* (Cugat autobiography)
79 *Fanfare for the ___* (P.D.Q. Bach work)
82 Cole Porter musical
83 Shy away from
84 Captain Picard's counselor
85 Minstrel show performer
86 Nixon's 1960 running mate
87 Since, to Burns

DOWN

1 Sort of steak
2 *___ Gold* (Peter Fonda film)
3 Foreshadows
4 Stands for
5 Gulf War missile
6 Jolson and Jarreau
7 Nephew of Abraham
8 Tinker-Chance connection
9 Benito Juárez, for one
10 Rat sung about by Michael Jackson
11 Author Levin
12 Family of "Bobby Hockey"
13 P.D.Q. Bach work
14 Of the hipbone
15 Mild cigar
20 Confined
24 Orienteer's reference
27 Chinese philosopher
28 *The Poseidon Adventure* producer Irwin
29 Good-for-nothing
30 French region
33 Grandmother of Juan Carlos
35 Assistance, so to speak
36 "Is that ___?"
37 Curriculum ___ (résumé)
38 *The Art of the ___* (P.D.Q. Bach work)
40 Got up
42 Iroquois' victims
43 Valley Forge accommodations
45 Home of a Biblical witch
46 Withdrew slowly
47 *Sleepless in Seattle* director
50 Florida city
53 Autocrat
55 NaOH solution
57 Usual
60 Farrow of *Be Kind Rewind*
62 Sound the alarm
63 Authoritative pronouncements
64 *Noises Off*, for one
65 Hawke of Hollywood
67 Brigham Young University home
69 Onetime *TV Guide* reviewer Cleveland
70 Honeydew, e.g.
71 "Sexy" Beatles girl
73 2,900, to Tiberius
75 Napoleonic ___
77 Ewe remark
78 Author Shirley ___ Grau
80 Like Carnaby Street fashions
81 Russian fighter plane

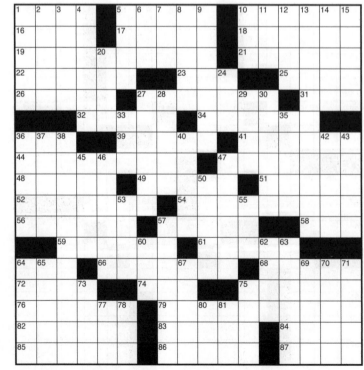

ANSWER, PAGE 57

Sherlock Holmes Novels

Sir Arthur Conan Doyle wrote only four full-length Sherlock Holmes novels; the other is *The Hound of the Baskervilles*.

ACROSS

1 Date of the Turin Winter Olympics
5 Onetime competitor of Freddie Laker
9 Abrade
14 Invent, as a phrase
15 Subtle atmosphere
16 Salutes
17 Sherlock Holmes novel
20 Fergie's first name
21 1973 PGA Rookie of the Year
22 Moslem name
23 Bunch of Boy Scouts
25 Big manufacturer of ATMs
26 Settled accounts
27 Steve Allen successor
28 Sounds of discomfort
29 Subject for Keats
30 Daughter of Hägar the Horrible

31 A, in Aachen
33 Sherlock Holmes novel
38 ___ a Wonderful Life
39 Tobies, for example
40 Cereal sound
42 Answer back
45 Deep cut
46 Rock singer Crofts
47 PC screen
48 *Lust for Life* author
50 Traveled a curved path
51 Australia's region
53 Trepidation
54 Sherlock Holmes novel
58 *The ___ House Rules*
59 Somali-born supermodel
60 Semester

61 Wiesbaden's state
62 To be, to Marie
63 "The ___ the limit!"

DOWN

1 Universal Studios' former owner
2 George S. Kaufman collaborator
3 Biotin's other name
4 Became accustomed (to)
5 Evan of Indiana
6 *Non* opposite
7 Prince Valiant's son
8 Brother of Olive Oyl
9 Title holder
10 Old-time exclamation

11 Under the weather
12 1985 Chevy Chase film
13 Fragrant compounds
18 Martin, to Emilio
19 Whisper sweet nothings
22 *The Simpsons* shop owner
23 Sharp taste
24 Hoffman Oscar film
27 Roots for Polynesians
28 Numero ___
30 Presidential monogram
31 Alphabetic quartet
32 "No ___, ands, or buts!"
34 Frozen water: German
35 English river

36 In trouble
37 George Clooney's aunt
41 Prof.'s degree, often
42 Rob Roy ingredient
43 Jughead's pal
44 War horses
45 One interested in net savings?
46 Preliminary manuscripts
48 Drum attachment
49 Shortened preposition
50 Gordon Shumway's other name
52 St. crossers
53 Highly rated
55 Paramedic: Abbr.
56 *Star Trek: The Next Generation* character
57 *Six ___ Riv Vu*

ANSWER, PAGE 59

Composer Portrayers

Others include Cary Grant (Cole Porter in 1946's *Night and Day*) and
Clifton Webb (John Philip Sousa in 1952's *Stars and Stripes Forever*).

ACROSS

1 *Enigma Variations* composer
6 Spanish misses: Abbr.
11 "Blame It on the ___ Nova"
16 Joe Buck's pal
17 17-syllable poem
18 Intrudes, with "in"
19 Billy Dee Williams (1977)
21 Action, so to speak
22 Road hazard
23 Country singer Gibbs
25 WWI German admiral
26 Frayed
29 Shortened conjunction
31 Seeks (to)
33 Elevs.
34 British record label
35 Alvah Roebuck partner
37 Their motto is "Can Do"
39 Gumshoe
40 Sportscaster Cross
41 Only crime mentioned in the U.S. Constitution
43 *Politically Incorrect* host
45 Nashville broadcast, for short
47 Ram's horn used in synagogues
50 City in Algeria
51 Nat King Cole (1958)
53 Nary a soul
54 Sequel designation, perhaps

56 One-on-one match
57 Pelota holder
58 *Oh, the Places You'll Go!* author
60 *Hollywood Squares* nonwinner
62 Get dressed, with "out"
63 Malcolm McDowell, in *Time After Time*
65 Clown device
67 *Bambi* deer
68 Spahn stat
69 *My Life as ___*
71 Charlottesville sch.
72 ___ Mawr
73 State flower of Utah
75 Become inedible
77 One way to vote
79 Like some dumbbells: Abbr.

56 One-on-one
81 Toralv Maurstad (1970)
86 *Superfly* star
87 Interminably
88 Larry Mahan's sport
89 Brash
90 Eye problems
91 Chessmaster from India

DOWN

1 Sounds of hesitation
2 Fond du ___, Wisconsin
3 Sporty Pontiac of yore
4 Sean of *Rudy*
5 Coll. military org.
6 "___ 'nuff!"
7 Toronto hoopster
8 Maj-jongg piece
9 Director Kurosawa

10 Daily event
11 Pellet projectiles
12 On the ___ (not speaking)
13 Don Ameche (1939)
14 Tampa neighbor
15 Size up
20 Yankee star Derek
24 Oscar-winning song from *Nashville*
26 Floor cleaner
27 1998 British Open winner
28 Richard Burton (1983)
30 Gypsy Rose Lee's sister June
32 Merit badge holder
35 Title for Michael Caine

36 Horst Buchholz (1972)
38 "April Love" singer
42 Sandberg of baseball
44 ___ nous (confidentially)
46 Advanced degs.
48 *Julius Caesar* hero
49 Subject of the biography *An American Hero*
51 Exerts
52 564, in old Rome
55 Cuba, *por ejemplo*
57 Barracks bed
59 Tourneys played at Arthur Ashe Stadium
61 He played Chan before Toler
63 '60s Screen Actors Guild president
64 Football player in a memorable Coke commercial
66 New Orleans school
70 Never-seen title character of the theater
72 "Ode on Venice" poet
74 Norwegian royal name
76 Actress Judith
78 Mogul Empire capital
80 Pulitzer's globetrotter
82 Hwys.
83 Bogie's *High Sierra* costar
84 Suffix for velvet
85 Ra or Helios

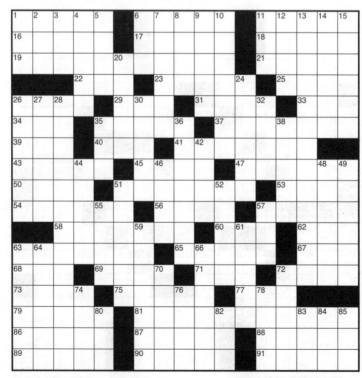

ANSWER, PAGE 61

Tall Structures

As of this writing, the world's tallest building is the Taipei 101 in Taipei, Taiwan.

ACROSS

1 Disraeli's title
5 Jai ___
9 Davis of *Cutthroat Island*
14 Duncan device
15 Apollo 11 name
16 *Siegfried* solos
17 The Empire State Building has 73 of them
19 Odets title character
20 Dubai ruler
21 Will Smith role
23 Service charge
24 Jellystone Park toon
28 The Angels' division
30 Metropolis newspaper
31 Tough going
33 Slow down, in mus.
34 Bar mitzvah officiator
36 Tavern phrase
39 Balanced
41 "When a body ___ ..."
43 Rainout preventer
44 Storm drain

46 Technical analyst's discovery
48 Clausewitz concern
49 Turkey's highest peak
51 Leblanc detective
53 Bobby McFerrin's collaborator on *Hush*
55 Capone's home circa 1935
57 In the style of
58 Superfund agcy.
60 Actress Skye
61 Major Burns expletive
63 Site of Europe's tallest building from 1990 to 2005
68 Pearl product
69 Cape Town cash
70 Mr. Rogers's first name

71 "He's Got the Whole World ___ Hands"
72 Fit to serve
73 Rock group from Sydney

DOWN

1 Pinkerton symbol
2 Popular ISP
3 Bread in a Reuben sandwich
4 Hippie happening
5 Battleground of 1862
6 *Arrowsmith* wife
7 *Why Is There ___?* (Cosby album)
8 The kid in "Here's looking at you, kid"
9 *Enterprise* shuttle craft

10 Palindromic preposition
11 World's tallest structure at the start of the 20th century
12 Thurmond and Archibald
13 So far
18 Winsor novel *Forever ___*
22 Little shaver
24 WWI battle site
25 Marie Osmond's real first name
26 Its official name is the Jefferson National Expansion Monument
27 Third Astaire/ Rogers film

29 Cosmetics applicator
32 Baptism, for example
35 Software test version
37 Hotpoint competitor
38 Javier ___ de Cuéllar
40 Caligula's nephew
42 Largest snake species
45 Memorable Brynner role
47 Imbibed
50 Some MTV music
52 Contemporary of Monica and Gabriela
53 New Age keyboardist
54 Faux fat brand
56 Hansen of NPR
59 Michael Jackson once wore one
62 Lockheed ___-Star
64 Wasn't colorfast
65 Caterer's container
66 Cornish ___ (cat breed)
67 Y.A. Tittle had 212 of them in his pro career

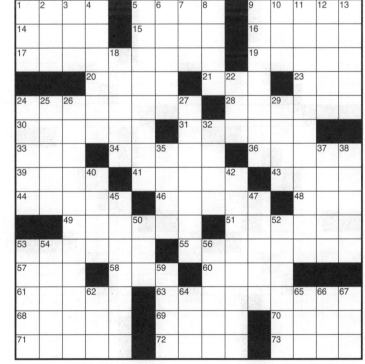

ANSWER, PAGE 63

College Team Nicknames

Others include Scarlet Knights (Rutgers),
Sun Devils (Arizona State), and Commodores (Vanderbilt).

ACROSS

1 *Guys and Dolls* character
6 Ancient Greek marketplace
11 Kitchen device
16 ___ hitch (type of knot)
17 Scrooge, for one
18 Presented itself
19 Louisiana-Lafayette
21 "Rudolph the Red-Nosed Reindeer" composer
22 Pop quartet's surname
23 Strain ___ gnat
24 Paradoxical question, in Zen
26 Prefix for picker
27 Poker winnings
28 Jai alai courts
30 "Too bad!"
31 Second British prime minister at Potsdam
32 Ishmael's ship
34 First recording superstar
37 Mayberry address abbr.
40 *Speed* vehicle
41 "Dilbert" character
42 Fish hawk
45 Sherlock's street
48 Isabella Rossellini's half-sister
49 California-Irvine
51 "Shine a Little Love" group
52 Activist with "Raiders"
54 #1 tune for Marty Robbins
55 Heavenly bodies
56 Former vitamin dosage: Abbr.

57 Louvre Pyramid architect
58 "The Sentimental Gentleman of Swing"
60 Nancy's pal
63 Like some mutual funds
66 Drink with a nose
67 Christmas liquors
70 Title for Evita: Abbr.
73 Edith ___ (Lily Tomlin character)
74 *The Nazarene* author
75 Hockey official
76 Beau for a doe
77 Calls for
79 Alabama
82 Pesetas' successors
83 Put back to zero, perhaps

84 Film role for Arnold
85 Lexmark competitor
86 Italian town of fiction
87 *Macbeth* or *Peter Grimes*

DOWN

1 Jettison
2 Crockett's last stand
3 Best-known synonymist
4 First car-rental company with airport outlets
5 Female pheasant
6 Ammonium nitrate + TNT
7 Demi Moore film of '97

8 The Buckeyes: Abbr.
9 *Hill Street Blues* cop played by Charles Haid
10 Insurance investigator's finding
11 Rhett's last word
12 Roth plan
13 Nebraska
14 Greenland language
15 Ready to go back to work
20 "Steamboat Willie," e.g.
25 Warbucks henchman, with "the"
28 Worth and Wayne: Abbr.
29 Maryland
30 Sea shade

31 Razor-billed bird
33 Low points
34 ___ Andy (*Show Boat* character)
35 Where most people live
36 Texas-San Antonio
38 Cheese made from goat's milk
39 Easter egg coverings
43 G to A, in music
44 Scorer of 1,281 career goals
46 Part of the East German–West German border
47 Hunky-dory
49 "To ___ and a bone ...": Kipling
50 *La Bohème* hero
53 Margin
55 Former California fort
59 Hemispheric alliance
60 George Gershwin's best-selling song in his lifetime
61 Police ID procedure
62 Cries of pain
64 Crew team
65 Deceives
68 Capital of Ghana
69 Modicum
70 *Go Eat Worms!* author
71 Trooper's tool
72 '60s NASA rocket
74 Trade org.
76 CD player button
78 "Inka Dinka ___"
80 *The Heart ___ Lonely Hunter*
81 Sergeant, for example: Abbr.

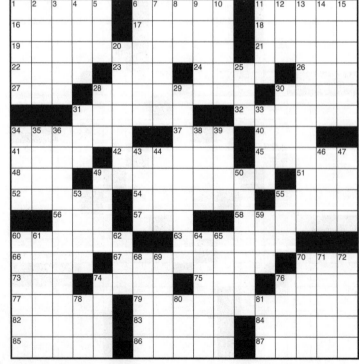

ANSWER, PAGE 57

48

Elvis Presley Films

Others include *King Creole* (1958),
It Happened at the World's Fair (1963), and *Clambake* (1967).

ACROSS

1 Nipsey Russell offering
5 One-pot dinner
9 *American Buffalo* playwright
14 Notions case
15 Bridget Fonda film of '87
16 Funt's order
17 Elvis film of '62
20 Mean look
21 Greek salad ingredient
22 Soviet news agency
23 Man Friday
25 Company whose name is pig Latin for an insect
27 Elvis film of '65
31 Program interrupters
34 Actor Estrada

35 Track window alternative: Abbr.
36 Tatum O'Neal Oscar role
38 Occupation
39 Figure skater Hughes
42 Yemen neighbor
43 Mythical sorceress
45 "Rumble in the Jungle" winner
46 Rat Pack nickname
47 Draft org.
48 Elvis film of '60
52 Throat invader
53 One of the casters of the Liberty Bell
54 Dog-license org.
57 Cardinal point
59 Last name of Archie girlfriend Veronica
63 Elvis film of '62

66 Walks heavily
67 "Age of Aquarius" musical
68 Half of a fluid ounce: Abbr.
69 Knuckleheads
70 Out of kilter
71 Waist neighbors

DOWN

1 Cribbage board inserts
2 Ear-related
3 Two-tone coin
4 *Happy Days* setting
5 Droop
6 Track bet
7 Irish Republic
8 Pidgeon or Payton
9 NYC sports venue
10 *Jaws* setting
11 Star in Cetus

12 Right-angle shapes
13 Thomas Hardy character
18 Svelte
19 Actor from India
24 Brit. medals
26 "I ___ Rock" (Paul Simon tune)
27 Nixon CIA director
28 First sign of the zodiac
29 Melon covers
30 James ___ Garfield
31 Fess up to
32 Wonder Woman alias
33 Ventriloquist ___ Wences
37 Sinclair Lewis novel
40 *Masterpiece Theatre* name
41 Suggestion

44 Part of ANC
49 He bought Metro Pictures in 1920
50 Hercule's creator
51 *Exodus* soundtrack composer Ernest
52 1992 British Open champ
54 Harry Callahan's employer: Abbr.
55 Ralph Lauren brand
56 Bull in a china shop
58 *Saint Joan* playwright
60 Figure skater Thomas
61 Sound of shock
62 Absolute rulers: Abbr.
64 "Wild Bill" Donovan's org.
65 Do one's best

ANSWER, PAGE 59

Civil War

1,520 Medals of Honor were awarded for service during the Civil War, about 45% of all the Medals of Honor awarded to date.

ACROSS

1 Oscar winner Hilary
6 Brigid O'Shaughnessy in *The Maltese Falcon*
11 Dumas character
16 Alphabetically, first name in Cooperstown
17 Southwestern plain
18 Onetime *Hollywood Squares* regular
19 Four of them remained with the Union
21 Lumberjacks, often
22 Home of the NHL Blues
23 Cool it
24 30-Across alternatives
26 ___ Championship (one of the majors)
27 R ___ "Robert"
28 Jazz singer Carmen
29 Daycare attendee
30 One in a cage
33 "Get lost!"
34 Poet Van Duyn
35 Where metacarpals are
36 Diamonds, in slang
37 Apt maiden name of Buzz Aldrin's mother
39 Cube man Rubik
40 NBC series since '75
41 *King Kong* star
44 Sinbad transport
45 Thomas Jackson's nickname
48 Bach's "Air ___ G String"
49 Shape-shifting Greek god
51 Jack-in-the-box part
52 It may be bleeped
53 Actor Schreiber
54 *Cheers* serving
55 Prefix for vascular
57 DC 100
59 King Abdullah II's capital
61 International education agency
62 Short putt
63 Robin's mother in *The World According to Garp*
64 Element's ID
65 5-Down's locale: Abbr.
66 Like some awakenings
67 ___ Pea (*Popeye* character)
68 Boot part
71 "Me no ___" (memorable review of *I Am a Camera*)
73 Admiral Farragut's flagship
76 Chief island of the Philippines
77 Hindu lute
78 *The Other Side of the Rainbow* author
79 Exhausted
80 Cable channel
81 Original Tin Man in *The Wizard of Oz*

DOWN

1 Guff
2 Cartoonist Kelly
3 Shrinking inland sea
4 Guy Fawkes Day mo.
5 120-member assembly
6 Site of the final Lincoln-Douglas debate
7 Affront
8 Puddy ___
9 4,840 square yards
10 Speakers' spots
11 ___ of mistaken identity
12 George Lucas's movie sound system
13 *Monitor/Merrimack* battle
14 The Beaver State
15 Moonlight or Kreutzer
20 Moves a muscle
25 Lemur or leopard
27 Likewise
28 Democratic presidential candidate in 1864
30 Dweeb
31 Faux pas
32 Annual award for the best Civil War scholarly work
33 ___ Fein
34 Trim the fairway
38 Shelley Duvall role of '80
40 Brillo competitor
41 Mood rings, in the '70s
42 Frolicsome
43 Major Internet portal
45 Call a bet
46 Pacific island nation
47 European capital, to natives
50 Third word of "America"
52 Nabisco brand
54 Title character's affliction in *The Bourne Identity*
55 More adorable
56 "Tall Paul" singer Funicello
57 "Suite: Judy Blue Eyes" composer Stephen
58 Relent
60 Gorgon of note
63 Vicksburg victor
64 Sentient
67 Roe source
68 *Flipper* producer
69 *Coffee, Tea ___?*
70 Plot in Genesis
72 Arroz ___ pollo
74 AT&SF stop
75 Watch pocket

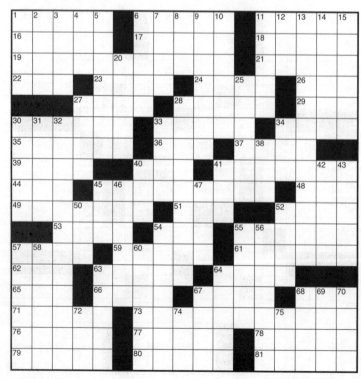

ANSWER, PAGE 61

Neil Simon

Neil Simon's real first name is Marvin.

ACROSS

1 Hal Roach's *Our* ___ comedies
5 Revolutionary War hero
9 Title character of a Menotti opera
14 Fictional lab assistant
15 Persian poet
16 Jazz pianist whose real first name is Armando
17 Neil Simon, for one
20 Jonny Quest's dog
21 *Good Housekeeping* offering
22 New England soda fountain
23 Cain's land of exile
25 Denise Crosby TV role Tasha ___
27 One of four Simon plays on Broadway in 1968
33 BPOE members

37 Meteorology device
38 Weather systems
39 Straight up
40 Flapjack franchises
41 A, as in Arles
42 Run amok
43 Gillette brand
44 Move slightly
45 Wisconsin birthplace of the GOP
46 Money-making operation
47 Simon screenplay of '79
49 Give it ___ (try)
51 ___ Na Na
52 Mideast bazaar
55 Metals in the rough
58 Wagner soprano
63 Simon play about Lewis and Clark

66 Packing heat
67 Video game invented by Nolan Bushnell
68 Small bills
69 Aggressive personality
70 Costner role
71 De Valera's country

DOWN

1 Bee Gees' surname
2 Taj Mahal locale
3 Fateful time in a Gary Cooper film
4 Diploma holder
5 Instruction books
6 GPs' gp.
7 Pringles competitor
8 Russian-born artist
9 Amtrak's fastest train
10 Extinct bird

11 Letters' partner
12 Dickens clerk
13 Wife of Jor-El
18 Kuwaiti currency
19 "First Lady of the American Theater"
24 Bob Dylan's birthplace
26 Director whose father was a painter
27 *Iliad* character
28 *Chicago Hope* actress
29 Doll up
30 Oil company founded by Bush Sr.
31 Ancient Greek region
32 Pipsqueaks
34 Left the ground
35 Punch sound, in comics

36 Pitman pro
42 Musical set at Rydell High
44 Derision
48 *All ___ Considered* (NPR program)
50 Cream-colored cheese
52 GNP, e.g.
53 *Driving Miss Daisy* playwright
54 Reagan HUD secretary
56 Network partly owned by Hearst
57 Mother Goose dwelling
59 *Peter and the Wolf* duck
60 Burt's *Stroker Ace* costar
61 *Your Erroneous Zones* author
62 To be: Latin
64 Bishop's domain
65 Alien-admission agcy.

ANSWER, PAGE 63

Sgt. Pepper Cover Subjects

Others include Oliver Hardy,
Albert Einstein, and Edgar Allan Poe.

ACROSS

1 Where Anne Frank hid
6 "The Lion of ___" (Haile Selassie)
11 Congress televiser
16 Like dishwater
17 Employment
18 Legend maker
19 *In Old Chicago* star
21 Sign of indifference
22 Nova Scotia clock setting: Abbr.
23 "Lord, is ___?": Matthew
24 Composer Rorem
25 Devoutness
26 *Mad About You* cousin
27 League of Women Voters founder
29 *A Bridge Too ___*
30 Litter member
32 "Jabberwocky" writer
39 Figure-eight halves
41 Expired
42 *Acoustic Soul* singer India.___
43 Opposite of paleo-
45 "Stupid ___" (Connie Francis tune)
47 *I ___ Fugitive From a Chain Gang*
48 1924 Olympics hero
54 Second-largest bird species
55 Romanov rulers
56 Alias initials
57 Robbins et al.

59 Type of vacuum tube
62 Moral code
66 *The Red Badge of Courage* author
69 Spouse of a countess
70 Lord's Prayer starter
71 Middle of the seventh century
73 Card game
74 Tout sheet listings
77 Word often following "long"
80 Čapek play
81 ___-Cat (winter vehicle)
82 Wolfpack member
83 '60s heavyweight champ
86 Nero's instrument
87 Watergate-implicated org.

88 *The Chevy Show* star
89 MI-to-ND road
90 Big name in hotels
91 Sweetie pie

DOWN

1 His last film was *Ghost Story*
2 KB competitor
3 Plaid patterns
4 Wall St. introduction
5 Pessimist
6 Europa circles it
7 The president is its honorary chairman
8 Tony Orlando's backup
9 Onetime *Time* film critic
10 *City Slickers* concern
11 One of the Magi

12 Apollo 7 commander
13 Word in Ivory Soap commercials
14 In ___ (stuck)
15 '50s Hungarian statesman
20 Footnote abbreviation
28 Airline bought by American
29 Daughter of Muhammad
31 Scopes Trial setting: Abbr.
33 Canine neighbor
34 Former French coins
35 Recipe units
36 Vocal
37 Lawn treatment
38 Goneril's father
40 Shipped out

44 Closemouthed one, so to speak
46 Wayne's nickname
48 Namath's first pro team
49 Leave out
50 Telejournalist Brit
51 Emulate Cassandra
52 10th-century explorer
53 Like the White Rabbit
58 Where Bing Crosby went to college
60 Scoutmaster, often
61 Do an NSC job
63 Roy Frowick's middle name
64 Hematite, for example
65 Star of the *Ocean's Eleven* remake
67 He directed his father and daughter in Oscar roles
68 Tishri preceder
72 From Mayo
74 Chinese cuisine tidbit
75 Bird seen in hieroglyphics
76 Ulster or mackintosh
77 *The Apostle* author
78 R-rated, perhaps
79 Liable to be drafted
84 Safety device
85 Cable network: Abbr.

ANSWER, PAGE 57

George Washington

Washington's second inaugural address in 1793 was just 135 words long—the shortest to date by far.

ACROSS

1 Unwoven fabric
5 Not oneself
8 He played Santa in *Elf*
13 Promontory Point locale
14 "In ___ penny ..."
15 Biblical land
16 *Earth in the Balance* author
17 King David Club administrator
18 Deck with cups and wands
19 Like Washington's two presidential elections
21 Form of oxygen
22 Fabray, familiarly
23 Actress Reid
25 Brought to naught
29 ___ *Zeppelin*
31 Star followers
35 Where Novi Sad is
37 Mysterious sightings
39 Hoodoo
40 Washington's first secretary of state
43 Sea eagle
44 Big name in dictionaries
45 "Well, ___!" ("Ain't you somethin'!")
46 Club fees
48 Pac-10 team
50 Dred Scott Decision chief justice
51 His theme was "Bubbles in the Wine"
53 Jamaican music
55 Sharon of Israel
58 Washington victory site of 1777
64 '30s dance
65 "Darling, Je Vous ___ Beaucoup"
66 Factotum
67 *Catching the Thanksgiving Turkey* painter
68 Healing plant
69 Peter Pan foe
70 *Basic Instinct* star
71 Gun the engine
72 Oregon, once: Abbr.

DOWN

1 Japanese delicacy
2 School attended by 007
3 Pasternak heroine
4 Consequently
5 Chinese export
6 Missus, in München
7 *Merry Wives of Windsor* character
8 "The Landlord of New York"
9 Gomer Pyle exclamation
10 Galba predecessor
11 Deep black
12 Be worthy of
14 Disaster-relief agcy.
20 Crow or Plains
24 Large union, for short
25 Spanish pronoun
26 Rajiv Gandhi's grandfather
27 Remote-control plane
28 Deep Blue developer
30 *Lost in Yonkers* star
32 Mark Twain character
33 Hollow mineral
34 "Cut that out!"
36 Not ___ (no one)
38 Washington State airport
41 His tag line was "I kid you not"
42 Former nutrient stat: Abbr.
47 Ann-Margret's homeland
49 *The Gods Themselves* author
52 *Family Ties* mom
54 Patella site
55 Charity
56 Civil unrest
57 Not ___ many words
59 Steam up
60 Orient
61 Magazine debut of 1923
62 North Sea feeder
63 Poetic adverb

ANSWER, PAGE 59

W.C. Fields Roles and Pseudonyms

Others include Ambrose Wolfinger (*The Man on the Flying Trapeze*),
Eustace McGargle (*Poppy*), and Egbert Sousé (*The Bank Dick*).

ACROSS

1 Manhattan variation
7 To start with
12 Bout enders
16 Symphony originally dedicated to Napoleon
17 Fred Astaire's birthplace
18 Mandlikova of tennis
19 Screenwriting pseudonym for *The Bank Dick*
22 Camera types: Abbr.
23 Podded plants
24 Ski lifts
25 ___ Coyote
27 Sioux City resident of song
28 *My Little Chickadee* role
36 They're green
37 Metric land measure
38 City founded by Pizarro
39 Keats, for one
40 In the thick of
41 County's capital
42 School literacy program
43 Role in *You're Telling Me*
48 ___ Khan
49 He beat Arthur at the 1972 U.S. Open

51 Semester
52 Sphere of influence
54 Home of Zeno
55 Coronado quest
56 *Lost in Space* mother
59 Role in *You Can't Cheat an Honest Man*
62 Ironside assistant
63 Tubs at the market
64 Essence of a Mae West invitation
67 *Sister Act* group
69 Kind of radio
73 Role in *It's the Old Army Game*
77 Gemayel of Lebanon
78 "Ready or not, ___ come!"

79 Is of use
80 Database function
81 Actress Paget
82 Thermopylae victor

DOWN

1 Dreamer's phenomena
2 Graduate degree exam
3 Danish physicist
4 Southwestern creeks
5 Start of the 4th qtr.
6 Verb for Popeye
7 WWI German planes
8 Turkish inn
9 ___ temperature (was ill)

10 Mares and ewes
11 ___ Mahal
12 Poe poem
13 Polynesian beverage
14 Unique individual
15 Be disrespectful
20 Certain Web surfer
21 Needle case
25 Minimal amounts
26 "May ___ frank?"
27 Malmö resident
28 French marking
29 Garibaldi, notably
30 Madman Muntz offerings
31 Traffic report details
32 Tampa paper
33 Sluggard

34 John Lennon album
35 Annoy
39 Bay window
40 Intention
44 Show contrition
45 Insignificant
46 Forehead
47 Qualifies for
50 Deed stipulation
53 "Oh, give ___ home ..."
56 Second Amendment word
57 Mimicry
58 Hope show sponsor
60 Done with
61 Owl
64 Freedom of the ___ (one of Wilson's Fourteen Points)
65 Neighbor of Dagwood
66 Mideast ruler
67 Canadian Indian
68 Neighbor of Dagwood
69 Winglike
70 CCCLIII tripled
71 Manicurist's tool
72 Pickle
74 Advanced deg.
75 *House of ___* (3-D film)
76 "___ Got a Crush on You"

ANSWER, PAGE 61

License Plate Slogans

Others include "Greatest Snow on Earth" (Utah),
"Land of Living Skies" (Saskatchewan), and "Keystone of the Pacific" (Okinawa).

ACROSS

1 Brewing ovens
6 *Top Hat* studio
9 Ran a tab
13 Something to sound
14 Actress Merkel
15 Freedom Ride organizer
16 Idaho
19 "Blue Clear Sky" singer George
20 One end of the Suez Canal
22 Poisonous snake
24 Pilot-licensing agcy.
25 ALCS month
26 Three, in Turin
27 Bloke
29 *Mary Tyler Moore Show* spinoff
31 "No ifs, ands, or ___!"
32 Port of Spain
34 Third tennis point
36 Alaska
42 One of a Puccini dozen
43 Future perfect, e.g.
44 Sean Connery, by birth
47 Buck Rogers colleague ___ Deering
50 Three-player card game
51 Dada painter
52 Part of VAT
53 Suffix for fool
55 Vicious of the Sex Pistols
56 Sitcom that Sondheim wrote scripts for
58 Creator of Moonbeam McSwine
60 Tennessee
64 Real estate ad abbreviation
65 Lady Bird successor
66 Historical trivia
67 "She loves you" follower
68 Monets and Manets
69 Special interest gps.

DOWN

1 Lummox
2 "Heart of Dixie": Abbr.
3 Miles Archer's partner
4 Harness race
5 Toon created by Belgian Pierre Culliford
6 Indonesian coin
7 Double Windsor, for one
8 Bran source
9 Work for eight
10 Speed-reading pro
11 Top 10 tune of '74
12 Great Sandy or Kalahari
17 Coal-rich German region
18 Six-time Preakness winner
21 DDE defeated him twice
22 Ad agency client: Abbr.
23 Pahlavi ruler
25 Nasal appraisal
28 Harbor guide
30 Garbage
31 Hard drive units
33 Use a ray gun
35 Boxer Tony Tubbs's nickname
37 Lincoln secretary of state
38 General Mills brand
39 "If I Didn't Care" singers
40 Actor Morales
41 Sent back: Abbr.
44 Matinee day: Abbr.
45 *The Bells of St. Mary's* star
46 Rebel against
48 Giants' #4
49 With the bow, in music
52 Agent's portion, at times
54 One third of "and so on"
57 Wild cat
58 Culture medium
59 School funding supporters
61 Saratoga Springs, for one
62 *12 Angry ___*
63 Tee preceder

ANSWER, PAGE 63

6

E	L	B	O	W		I	T	H	A	C	A		A	C	T	E
T	O	I	L	E		C	R	I	S	I	S		L	A	I	D
C	O	O	L	T	H	O	U	G	H	T	S		G	R	E	G
E	T	N	A		O	N	T	H	E		G	E	R	R	Y
T	E	D		S	U	S	H	I		S	C	A	R	Y	
C	R	I	S	P	S		Q	U	E	L	L		I	S	H	
	E	R	E	C	T		P	A	U	L	A	N	K	A	
M	C	F	L	Y		P	E	G	S		N	O	R	G	A	Y
A	C	R	E		R	U	N	N	I	N	G		D	O	T	E
G	L	I	N	D	A		A	U	D	I		B	E	N	E	S
E	V	E	A	R	D	E	N		E	X	C	O	N	
S	I	D		L	A	T	T	E		H	O	T	E	L	S
	M	E	A	R	A		A	U	R	A	S		S	A	P
F	R	E	D	O		A	S	T	O	R		A	T	N	O
L	O	A	D		D	O	N	T	L	O	O	K	B	A	C	K
A	N	T	I		E	Y	E	L	E	T		T	U	T	E	E
B	A	S	E		A	L	W	A	Y	S		S	T	E	R	N

11

T	E	N	D		G	E	A	R		R	A	I	S	A
A	M	I	E		U	L	N	A		E	P	S	O	M
T	I	N	K	A	T	O	N	K	A	T	R	I	B	E
A	L	E	A	S	T		S	E	R	T		S	S	N
	L	I	E	D		S	L	O	T	
F	L	U	B	A	D	U	B		I	N	O	U	Y	E
E	E	R		R	A	G	S		A	D	A	M
T	O	B	E		L	A	N	E	S		D	A	L	I
I	N	A	N		I	N	F	O		L	I	T
D	E	N	I	R	O		F	R	E	C	K	L	E	S
	D	O	N	S		G	N	A	R	
A	A	A		M	E	T	E		A	V	A	T	A	R
B	U	F	F	A	L	O	B	O	B	S	M	I	T	H
B	R	A	I	N		M	A	I	L		E	T	T	E
Y	A	R	N	S		P	Y	L	E		R	O	N	A

16

M	A	Z	E	S		M	M	D	C	L		D	W	E	L	T
R	E	U	E	L		A	L	E	R	O		O	R	D	E	R
B	I	L	L	Y	W	I	L	D	E	R		M	Y	W	A	Y
I	O	U	S		I	D	E	A	M	E	N		A	R	M
G	U	S		Y	E	S		L	E	N	A	H	O	R	N	E
	D	E	N		B	U	S		M	E	N	D	
A	P	A	R	T		T	I	S		W	I	D	M	A	R	K
T	O	N	Y		A	E	R		B	O	B	D	Y	L	A	N
O	L	D		V	L	A	D		A	R	I	A		B	T	U
M	Y	R	N	A	L	O	Y		U	S	A		F	E	E	T
S	P	E	A	R	E	R		A	G	E		M	E	E	S	E
	P	R	I	G		S	C	H		W	I	Z	
C	A	R	Y	G	R	A	N	T		P	O	D		F	A	Q
E	K	E		O	L	O	R	O	S	O		R	A	G	U
L	I	V	I	A		F	R	E	D	A	S	T	A	I	R	E
E	R	I	C	S		R	E	S	I	T		W	I	L	E	E
B	A	N	K	S		E	S	S	E	S		O	L	S	E	N

20

P	E	A	L	E		G	A	M	M	A		S	W	I	F	T
O	L	M	A	N		I	L	I	A	D		A	E	R	I	E
G	E	O	R	G	E	B	U	R	N	S		F	E	V	E	R
O	M	S	K		T	I	M	O	N		T	A	P	I	R	S
	C	A	L		A	F	A	R		N	Y	E	
A	G	G	I	E		L	A	M		R	U	I	N	G	
L	A	R	O	S	A		M	A	Z	E	S		A	B	A	T
P	L	A	N	T	S		B	L	E	U		O	B	E	S	E
H	E	N		A	L	F	L	A	N	D	O	N		R	S	T
A	N	D	E	S		J	I	M	I		R	E	E	L	E	R
S	A	M	S		D	O	N	U	T		B	I	K	I	N	I
	A	S	N	E	R		D	H	L		L	E	N	T	S
E	L	M		A	N	D	S		A	I	L	
T	H	O	R	N	Y		W	A	L	T	Z		A	S	A	P
H	A	S	A	T		R	O	S	E	K	E	N	N	E	D	Y
I	S	E	R	E		T	R	A	D	E		I	N	T	E	L
C	A	S	E	S		E	D	N	A	S		P	A	I	N	E

24

A	R	E	N	A		S	U	M	A	C		M	Y	W	A	Y
T	O	N	E	R		S	K	O	S	H		C	E	A	S	E
T	U	T	T	I	F	R	U	T	T	I		A	S	T	I	N
E	R	A	S	E	R		L	E	A	C	H		D	E	F	S
S	K	I		L	A	P	E	L		H	O	M	E	R	
T	E	L	E		N	I	L		C	I	N	N	A	M	O	N
	M	A	C	N	E	I	L		D	O	R	E	M	I	
C	A	P	U	L	E	T		N	A	S	A		L	A	X
A	L	I	S	T		O	N	E	P	M		E	C	O	N	O
N	I	N		V	S	O	P		A	N	T	O	N	I	N
A	B	A	C	U	S		S	T	O	R	I	E	S	
L	I	C	O	R	I	C	E		R	T	S		A	C	C	T
	O	M	E	G	A		G	E	S	S	O		H	A	H
P	O	L	O		N	U	K	E	S		A	R	C	A	N	A
O	H	A	R	A		C	O	T	T	O	N	C	A	N	D	Y
E	N	D	O	R		U	N	T	E	R		A	N	G	L	E
T	O	A	S	T		S	A	Y	S	O		S	T	E	E	R

28

C	A	N	S	T		T	O	R	C	H		B	O	U	T	S
A	M	O	R	E		E	N	O	L	A		E	N	N	U	I
R	E	F	O	R	M	A	T	I	O	N		A	L	F	R	E
I	N	E		R	C	C	O	L	A		C	R	Y	I	N	G
B	R	A	N	A	G	H		K	R	O	C		N	A	E
S	A	R	A		W	E	A	R		A	M	A	T	I	
	S	M	I	R	C	H		N	A	T	A	S	H	A
M	O	H	A	I	R		R	E	A	D		C	H	U	M
B	R	O		L	E	N	I	N	G	R	A	D		E	L	I
A	C	R	E		E	D	I	E		B	E	A	D	L	E
S	A	N	T	A	F	E		S	N	A	I	L	S	
	S	A	V	E	D		H	A	I	G		T	O	M	S
I	C	I		I	D	Y	L		R	A	P	A	N	U	I
M	A	G	M	A	S		A	R	A	B	I	A		E	R	E
B	I	N	E	T		A	P	O	C	A	L	Y	P	T	I	C
E	R	A	T	O		S	E	L	I	G		N	E	W	E	L
D	O	L	O	R		S	L	E	D	S		E	C	O	L	E

32

```
SMUTS CROSS SHAFT
LANAI TARPS HENIE
ITISCERTAIN EAGLE
PASSIM ANN CARLIN
   ELMO GOTO SEAS
BSA YESDEFINITELY
ANDS TAI FORD
SEOUL KAN OTELLO
REPLYHAZYTRYAGAIN
ARTURO CII GABLE
   INTO TAC NOLA
DONTCOUNTONIT REM
OREO REAR TROD
DISUSE SAO CLOTHO
GOTTI ASISEEITYES
ELLEN RINSE FERAL
REEDS ASSOC ERATO
```

36

```
HELP ANEGG CHANEL
ELUL LEARY BULOVA
ASIA PETERUSTINOV
ROSY EDITOR DEKE
SLED RITA IGO TER
   ROOT LAINE
ASAHI GENEHACKMAN
BMI LAIDON NEGATE
YOND MAGINOT SGTS
STEREO ARIOSE GIT
MERYLSTREEP EPICS
   SHOES PERE
STN IZE TELL USMC
TIOS NARNIA SMEE
ANTHONYQUINN SILL
GEMINI USAGE ITBE
GSEVEN ASCOT AHAB
```

40

```
IDO PORTIA SCOPES
SET ALEUTS TACOMA
ANE SALVATIONARMY
BALLS ASIMOV TAS
ELLE UAL RAGAS
LIONSCLUB ESHARP
   DELA ARMS AMIA
ASP LAB PEA EMBAR
SCREENACTORSGUILD
SOAPS MOI CEY TSO
OUTS RATS OOPS
CREOLE MINUTEMEN
   MIDST TIL LEDA
OER THRUSH DALIS
PRINCEOFWALES OTS
ELISHA TICTAC TOA
RESAID SMARTS TRU
```

44

```
TUBA SALEM BIONIC
BLOB CLOVE ERROLL
OEDIPUSTEX NARNIA
NEEDED RIM SOAR
ESSEN LASCALA NCO
   STEAL APOLLO
AVG NOLAN USENET
FIREWATER ETAGERE
ATONE SNOOP CUTIN
CAUDATE SCHLEPTET
TENONS TEARY ESS
   DREAMY LOEWE
FER DRIPPAN ADAMS
ATOM AIR CRIMEA
RHUMBA COMMONCOLD
CANCAN AVOID TROI
ENDMAN LODGE SYNE
```

48

```
SARAH AGORA DICER
CLOVE MISER AROSE
RAGINCAJUNS MARKS
AMES ATA KOAN NIT
POT FRONTONS AHME
   ATTLEE PEQUOD
CARUSO RFD BUS
ASOK OSPREY BAKER
PIA ANTEATERS ELO
NADER ELPASO ORBS
   RDA PEI DORSEY
SLUGGO NOLOAD
WINE WASSAILS SRA
ANN ASCH REF STAG
NEEDS CRIMSONTIDE
EUROS RESET CONAN
EPSON ADANO OPERA
```

52

```
ATTIC JUDAH CSPAN
SOAPY USAGE ACURA
TYRONEPOWER SHRUG
AST ITI NED PIETY
IRA CATT FAR
RUNT LEWISCARROLL
ESSES RANOUT ARIE
   NEO CUPID AMA
JOHNNYWEISSMULLER
EMU TSARS AKA
TIMS TRIODE ETHIC
STEPHENCRANE EARL
   OUR DCLI LOO
PICKS AGO RUR SNO
UBOAT SONNYLISTON
PIANO CREEP SHORE
USTEN HYATT HONEY
```

7

```
LIBRA ■ MARSH ■ TNT
ANAIS ■ ELITE ■ YOU
DCLVI ■ RIGOR ■ SON
SALEMOREGON ■ ONE
■ ■ ROLY ■ GAINES
BEHAVE ■ ACENT ■
ACE ■ AERO ■ DEGAS
CHEYENNEWYOMING
HOPES ■ YALU ■ FAT
■ ATRAS ■ KNOTTS
JETHRO ■ SOAP ■
EVA ■ AUSTINTEXAS
LIN ■ GREEN ■ INERT
LAG ■ OKING ■ VENAL
ONO ■ NESTS ■ ERATO
```

12

```
NICAD ■ MACON ■ HAWKS
ASONE ■ GROVE ■ LLANO
CANDLEMAKER ■ HOSEA
RADIUM ■ BIRDHUNTER
ECO ■ DANSE ■ ENGELS
■ DENY ■ PHAT ■
ASHE ■ USSTEEL ■ CLOG
SPENCE ■ OURS ■ MAEVE
TRAVELINGSALESMAN
RAVEL ■ BNAI ■ ESTATE
OYER ■ GAETANO ■ LYES
■ BURT ■ APSE ■
SAHARA ■ FSTOP ■ LAB
STONEMASON ■ LADIDA
GRADY ■ WAGONDRIVER
TERRE ■ ENERO ■ TOILE
SEDER ■ SAYER ■ ANDES
```

17

```
MAJOR ■ ALSOP ■ MST
BWANA ■ LETBY ■ RHO
ALWAYSFIRST ■ MUD
SSS ■ BALSA ■ HEXED
■ AURA ■ DAIRY ■
BOBCRANE ■ TARZAN
ALIEN ■ DUNES ■ PRE
RIGS ■ BORON ■ STUV
EVA ■ MANOR ■ BELLE
REPEAL ■ STREAKER
■ RENKO ■ HOST ■
SEIKO ■ COSTS ■ FSU
ARC ■ WITHTHENEWS
HMO ■ AGENA ■ LOMAN
LAT ■ ROTOR ■ LLAMA
```

21

```
NCAA ■ SHEIK ■ AJAR
EARN ■ RINSO ■ LOBO
THEDAILYPROPHET
SNARL ■ LAYER ■ NTH
■ EASY ■ ABC ■
SAFIRE ■ VANALLEN
IAL ■ MUIR ■ CEASE
GRYFFINDORHOUSE
MOIRA ■ DODO ■ RED
ANNARBOR ■ OCEANS
■ TRE ■ AMID ■
RAY ■ ONION ■ TWEED
YEARWITHTHEYETI
ARMY ■ NONET ■ NEON
NOSE ■ GROSS ■ NENE
```

25

```
HIGHC ■ BARB ■ SPAM
ARRAU ■ ESAU ■ TONE
TROLL ■ NOUN ■ ALTA
■ WOLFJFLYWHEEL
■ ELI ■ AOL ■
TULANE ■ SAND ■ UPA
ATAN ■ SCAN ■ EASES
HUGOZHACKENBUSH
ORONO ■ ICAN ■ LATE
ENS ■ NONO ■ TAYLOR
■ SKA ■ DRJ ■
RUFUSTFIREFLY
EGAD ■ ELLA ■ OSOLE
ALLA ■ REEK ■ YAYAS
RYAN ■ SADE ■ TTOPS
```

29

```
AMFM ■ SOOT ■ ABDUL
BOLA ■ ANKH ■ ZLOTY
BOAC ■ LEIA ■ TUNER
EDGRIMLEY ■ ERASE
■ AGAL ■ ETC ■
ADMEN ■ AFRO ■ BUSS
LOA ■ ACME ■ PRINCE
ISNTTHATSPECIAL
BELIZE ■ CASE ■ TRI
IDYL ■ ASHY ■ CDEFG
■ OPT ■ OAHU ■
SPITZ ■ JONLOVITZ
ARNAZ ■ ORAL ■ ADEE
NEGRI ■ HERA ■ LEEK
SPATE ■ NOAH ■ LANE
```

33

```
SHED  BASTE  NOEL
HALO  ACTII  ARTE
USSR  FEIGN  TETE
THEIRFINESTHOUR
    SHINE  TOA
PARDON   LEONARD
IDEAS  CHAIN  ROO
EDDY  THORN  TILL
RUY  SHEIK  CREEP
SPENCER   SHILOH
   OAF  CSPAN
HONORARYCITIZEN
AVON  TORUN  DOLE
LISA  EMILE  ALAN
EDEN  SELLS  DALE
```

37

```
REV  ACME  ABBOTT
ORO  MOAB  NEARER
MINDYOUR  GRANDY
ACTI  MOPSY  EIS
NIRVANA  ATL  RUT
IDA  GLUES  GYMS
ALPINE  USAGE
 EPLURIBUSUNUM
  ISSEI  FISTIC
ESTE  VENAL  TSR
AAA  IZE  ARTDECO
STU  PEROT  ERAS
TOPHAT  BUSINESS
ORIANA  IRAQ  RTE
NINJAS  EELS  SSS
```

41

```
FUJI  NCOS  IPSO
EROS  AARP  NIELS
SIGOURNEYWEAVER
SSS  HITS  ARNESS
   AUTO  ALTO
BARBRASTREISAND
OSHEA  RASA  LAO
NEIL  ABABA  DIDI
DAN  BEAM  SEVEN
STEVENSPIELBERG
   ARES  SPOT
GIANNI  SHOT  HMS
ALFREDHITCHCOCK
OKAYS  UTAH  XRAY
 ARNE  HERS  LANE
```

45

```
MMVI  BOAC  CHAFE
COIN  AURA  HAILS
ASTUDYINSCARLET
 SARAH  TOMKITE
AHMED  TROOP  NCR
PAID  PAAR  UGHS
URN  HONI  EIN
 THESIGNOFFOUR
 ITS  MUGS  POP
SASS  GASH  DASH
CRT  STONE  ARCED
OCEANIA  ALARM
THEVALLEYOFFEAR
CIDER  IMAN  TERM
HESSE  ETRE  SKYS
```

49

```
POEM  STEW  MAMET
ETUI  ARIA  SMILE
GIRLSGIRLSGIRLS
SCOWL  FETA  TASS
   AIDE  EBAY
HARUMSCARUM  ADS
ERIK  OTB  ADDIE
LINE  SARAH  OMAN
MEDEA  ALI  DINO
SSS  FLAMINGSTAR
   FROG  STOW
SPCA  EAST  LODGE
FOLLOWTHATDREAM
PLODS  HAIR  TBSP
DODOS  AWRY  HIPS
```

53

```
FELT  OFF  ASNER
UTAH  FORA  SHEBA
GORE  ELAL  TAROT
UNANIMOUS  OZONE
   NAN  TARA
UNDID  GRAF  MAGI
SERBIA  UFOS  HEX
THOMASJEFFERSON
ERN  NOAH  LADIDA
DUES  UCLA  TANEY
   WELK  SKA
ARIEL  PRINCETON
LINDY  AIME  AIDE
MOSES  ALOE  SMEE
STONE  REV  TERR
```

8

```
GRAIL SAMBA THATS
HINDU ENIAC HELIO
OFTIMEANDTHERIVER
ULE IDLEST LUNATE
LESSEN STLEO LRON
     EROS EXILE
OLIVERTWIST OINKS
KANE TABS CINEMA
ATL BOBCOSTAS HAS
PIEPAN LEAN ERRS
INTEL BLACKBEAUTY
     TIARA EELS
BOAR HONDO REEBOK
ACTONE GENERA UNE
THECOMPLEATANGLER
ERIKS AERIE ORGAN
SENSE MYERS REELS
```

13

```
TOSCA SEMIS ALP
ONEAM SLOTH LEE
PENSYLVANIA LIE
PATE YANK SMEAL
SLAYTON SATAN
   ANDA BARTON
PULPS ICAL COLA
OPEL ONCUE IWAS
NOVA CEES KENYA
GRINCH LTJG
  TEASE ROBERTS
GRITS AVIA DARE
AEC PASSANDSTOW
LSU ELTON REEVE
ETS RASPS ELDER
```

18

```
ELLER ENGEL JAPAN
WEARY DELTA IDAHO
ERNIENEVERS MILES
LOCK ARISES HOMME
LYE PULLS IOUS
  ADOSE TERN JAI
 SLATE ISH STEAMS
TOWN ALTHEA EMCEE
INOIL AHEAD RAKER
TORSO GIBSON INRE
ARTHUR NAP ELLIS
NAH GEEK EPISC
   SEAN DELHI KAN
PLATH TEETER ELLE
RILER RICHGOSSAGE
IMPEI ARONI SQUAD
GEORG PEROT ESSES
```

22

```
WHAT MMCV APT NIL
HALE CERF NRA ONO
IDONTKNOW DOC ODE
LOU OEUF TOMORROW
ENDORA THEROBE
  CCNY OAR ENCS
SMITH ARM AILERON
TODAY LIES BLEEPS
OVO BECAUSE WHY
REISER ELMO ATEIN
MODELAS OSS LILAC
 NONE CAN ACHT
  SCARLET LIOTTA
NINETIES ITAR BUD
ADE ORA IDONTCARE
TEX REM TALC DRIP
OAT SSS ALLY ISNT
```

26

```
RAINS MAFIA AMNIO
AGLET CRIST BRONX
GUADALCANAL BETSY
SAY NUCLEI BEDBUG
  ALG SAGO ARE
SCARE ANTHONYEDEN
LANCEITO DOER
ENG NAFTA AGAVE
DWIGHTDEISENHOWER
SEENO EATME ARA
  AWAY RICHARDS
PEARLHARBOR EDDIE
RUN ATOI RNS
ODDJOB METHOD OHO
SOREN HARRYTRUMAN
IREST UNCAP ITALY
TASSO MYEYE XEROX
```

30

```
TAMMY HADJI YAWLS
ALAMO ALOAN ATHOL
SLIMY NEWYORKLIFE
KELLOGGS LIES TAD
SYS MRS PELE PETS
  RAI GIN DISC
FAWN SHALOM MIAMI
ADOS HILL IMA SAD
LMN PANASONIC TRI
LID EMT BMOC CLIO
STEEL SQUASH SENT
  RITA URN AKA
GABS STAY JED RAS
ARR CARR HALLMARK
BEECHNUTGUM AEIOU
OMAHA SERGE NASAL
RYDER TREES GNARL
```

34

```
MAPLE SUMAC BOWES
ATEAT ERICA BRAVA
GRAPHICARTS CATES
IER NATL TEA NENE
CELTICS AWISH RTS
    ECO ETONIANS
SKED CATH FRAKES
CELS CAULKS DEIST
RAE GARDENING ITO
INCUR PETITE KNEW
PUTNAM ISAW OGEE
  RESEARCH HEF
PHI SILOS MADISON
ROCK RHO HARI ELO
ISIAH INSECTSTUDY
AETNA RETRY OSSIE
MAYER TYPES NOSES
```

38

```
FEMUR ERIC FLUFFS
AMANA LULU ROBERT
SIDEWINDER INOUYE
OLE TIETAC NADER
   ASSN TAROT
OVERLOOKHOTEL JAR
RESNIK HARSH ALA
ESTEE LAN EER ZIP
SPA STANDBYME ZAP
TET TYR SUE CHASE
ERE CABER SIEGEL
SSS PHILTRUMPRESS
   FIONA NEED
SEALE ENTAIL CII
ALHIRT CASTLEROCK
PLANCK HOSE TYPEE
SESTET ESTD CESTA
```

42

```
SAHIB ALIBI BOBBY
PLUTO BIDON CREED
ADMIRALBYRD DEEDS
MAE DIABLO LEO
   JERZY DCI VIS
NOMINEE WILEYPOST
USCG IONA MALTA
SEC BANDB INCISOR
 AMELIAEARHART
RERAISE GAELS ERE
ACTIN COOS BAER
JOHNGLENN MATADOR
ANY ESE FAGIN
   ZOT CALLAS FRO
LIVER NEWYORKMETS
BLAKE ONHER EASEL
JONES STORY TASSO
```

46

```
ELGAR SRTAS BOSSA
RATSO HAIKU BUTTS
SCOTTJOPLIN STEPS
   ICE TERRI SPEE
WORN THO AIMS HTS
EMI SEARS SEABEES
TEC IRV TREASON
MAHER OPRY SHOFAR
ORAN WCHANDY NONE
PARTII DUEL CESTA
  DRSEUSS XOO TOG
HGWELLS STILT ENA
ERA ADOG UVA BRYN
SEGO SPOIL NAY
TENLB EDVARDGRIEG
ONEAL NOEND RODEO
NERVY STYES ANAND
```

50

```
SWANK ASTOR ATHOS
AARON LLANO CHARO
SLAVESTATES AXMEN
STL STOP ATMS PGA
  ASIN MCRAE TOT
TELLER SCRAM MONA
WRISTS ICE MOON
ERNO SNL FAYWRAY
ROC STONEWALL ONA
PROTEUS LID OATH
 LIEV ALE CARDIO
SENS AMMAN UNESCO
TAP GLENN ATNO
ISR RUDE SWEE TOE
LEICA USSHARTFORD
LUZON SITAR TORME
SPENT AANDE EBSEN
```

54

```
ROBROY FIRST TKOS
EROICA OMAHA HANA
MAHATMAKANE JEEVES
SLRS OKRAS TBARS
   WILEE SUE
CUTHBERTJTWILLIE
ENVIERS ARE LIMA
ODIST AMID SEAT
RIF SAMBISBEE AGA
ILIE TERM AMBIT
ELEA ORO MAUREEN
LARSONEWHIPSNADE
   EVE OLEOS
SEEME CHOIR AMFM
ELMERPRETTYWILLIE
AMIN HEREI AVAILS
SORT DEBRA XERXES
```

9

```
A B C S . L A K . B U L L E T
G I U L I A N I . A M E R C E
C O L O S S A L . U S T O U R
Y S L . S T I N G S . I N S P
. . O U R S . O C A T . . .
G U I N E A . J O H N B U L L
I R M A . D O U G . K E N Y A
A I T . M A M M O T H . D I R
N A H U M . A B L E . R U N G
T H E P I A N O . R E N E G E
. . F I F I . K R I S . . .
M E I R . G S T A A D . F L U
E D K O C H . S U P E R I O R
A G E N D A . P A I R I N G S
N E A T E N . S I N . M E S A
```

14

```
B A S I S . V I L M A . A S P E R
R O O S T . I D E A L . N O L T E
O R L O N . S E A N C O N N E R Y
A T E M . S I E S T A S . A D E S
C A M E L O T . E R N E S T . .
H E N R Y F O N D A . E A R L E
. . N A R Y . S P A . I A N
A W A R D . M O O S E . A C I D
S Y L V E S T E R S T A L L O N E
S E I S . L A T K A . U T H E R
E T C . F A B . K A T E . .
S H E B A . C L A R K G A B L E
. . B A A B A A . M O O C H E R
I M U S . M A R B L E S . T U N A
S O P H I A L O R E N . P I T T S
P R I O R . E L E N I . T O T I E
Y E N T E . R E A T A . A N O L D
```

19

```
K I T E . A M E N . S H E B A
I D O L . N C A A . H A R E M
N L R B . O A R S . E R N I E
G E N E K R U P A . I R O N S
. . W A L . L I L Y . . .
C I S C O K I D . M A J O R S
O N I O N . F E T E . A R E A
L U L U . A F L A T . M O L L
I S A N . M E I R . D E N I S
N E S T L E . S A R A S O T A
. . B O X Y . N E T . . .
L A L A W . A R T I E S H A W
A R O S E . L O I S . H O B O
M O B I L . T O N E . O S L O
A N S E L . A M O R . W E E D
```

23

```
C A S K . S W A P S . A N A T
A N C E . H E M I N . S E R A
B E I N G A L O N E . S W I G
O A F . E N T R . E M O T E S
T R I L O G Y . C Z E C H . .
. . A S H . B O E R . I B M
K E L P . A U E L . C O N T I
C R O S S I N G B R I D G E S
A N N E S . D A Y O . I S N T
R E G . G M E N . S S S . .
. . W A T E R . M A L T E S E
P R O U S T . L A L O . L A D
Y A R D . E V E R Y T H I N G
R U D I . R O D I N . I O T A
E L S E . S W A N N . S T A R
```

27

```
H O E R . U R L S . P E D A L
E L S E . R I O T . O U I J A
R E A D I N G R A I L R O A D
D O U B T . H E L D . E R R S
. . A T W T . L O C K . . .
B A E R . E S S O . C A P R A
E R R O L L . K N O X . E O M
T E N N E S S E E A V E N U E
E N S . T H A I . K I T T E N
L A T C H . B N A I . H A N D
. . H E R A . S E T I . . .
R A J A . U T A H . I O W A N
E L E C T R I C C O M P A N Y
B O T H A . N E A T . I R K S
S E T A T . I S N T . A S H E
```

31

```
B L A N C . J O L T . B T U S
R O V E R . O R E O . L I S T
A C E L A . D E M O . I N S O
C A R L Y S I M O N . G A R P
. . O W E . N I G H T . . .
A R S E N E . S T E M . U M A
L A H R . E V E R . A A R O N
O V E N . P E L E E . U N I T
H E R O N . N E E D . E E R O
A N Y . A L E S . W A R R E N
. . L A P A Z . H I D . . .
U P C S . D U R A N D U R A N
H A R P . D E E D . A T O N E
O B O E . E L L E . M A S O N
H A W N . R A Y S . S H A N E
```

35

```
S E R I F   C H O W   C L I P
A G E N A   H O P E   H I V E
B A N D B   A B E L   E M I T
E D D Y A R N O L D   T O N E
      R A G       S A S S Y
S M O K E Y   A S C O T
P A R I S   M I N I S K I R T
A N A T   L I L A C   I T A R
M I N T J U L E P   S N A K E
    Y U C K Y   W E S S E X
C R O W N     F A A
R A C E   E R N E S T T U B B
E T A L   B O O R   T O P O L
T E L L   B D R M   L Y C R A
E R A S   S E M I   E S S E S
```

39

```
L A M E   A M I E S   I B E T
I G O R   D O N A T   D A L I
M E X I C O C I T Y   I R A N
A N I T A   S T I R   A C M E
S T E R E O   T O R M E
      E N D E R   N A I L E D
M A M A   I D O S   S N O W Y
A R E   A N T W E R P   N E E
W O L F S   V E T O   S A S S
R O B R O Y   R H O D A
    O A K E S     F E L D O N
F A U N   L U I S   N I O B E
L U R K   L O S A N G E L E S
A R N O   O M E G A   R E S T
B A E Z   W I E S T   I D E S
```

43

```
V A P O R   C X C I I   W J M
E V I T A   A F U S S   H A I
L A N E S   M I L L E   O N E
C L A R A P E L L E R   P E N
R O T I   O R E   S E E P
O N A   C O A S T     M E A D
    D U D   L E C A R R E
L I T E L L A   C U B I S T S
T R A P P E R   G E L
S E C T   P E T E R   A M Y
    O H O H   C O N   S L O E
K G B   S E S A M E S E E D S
A R E   A L A R M   H E X E S
N I L   G O T T I   E M I L E
E N L   E S S E X   A S S T S
```

47

```
E A R L   A L A I   G E E N A
Y O Y O   N E I L   A R I A S
E L E V A T O R S   L E F T Y
    E M I R   A L I   F E E
Y O G I B E A R   A L W E S T
P L A N E T   O R D E A L
R I T   R A B B I   O N T A P
E V E N   M E E T A   D O M E
S E W E R   T R E N D   W A R
    A R A R A T   A R S E N E
Y O Y O M A   A L C A T R A Z
A L A   E P A   I O N E
N E R T S   F R A N K F U R T
N A C R E   R A N D   F R E D
I N H I S   O N E A   I N X S
```

51

```
G A N G   H A L E   A M A H L
I G O R   O M A R   C O R E A
B R O A D W A Y T H E A T E R
B A N D I T   S E A L   S P A
      N O D   Y A R
P L A Z A S U I T E   E L K S
R A D A R   L O W S   N E A T
I H O P S   U N E   G O A P E
A T R A   S T I R   R I P O N
M I N T   C H A P T E R T W O
    A G O     S H A
S U K   O R E S   I S O L D E
T H E S U N S H I N E B O Y S
A R M E D   P O N G   O N E S
T Y P E A   N E S S   E I R E
```

55

```
O A S T S   R K O   O W E D
A L A R M   U N A   C O R E
F A M O U S P O T A T O E S
    S T R A I T   R E D S E A
A S P   F A A   O C T   T R E
C H A P   R H O D A   B U T S
C A D I Z   F O R T Y
T H E L A S T F R O N T I E R
    O P E R A   T E N S E
S C O T   W I L M A   S K A T
A R P   T A X   E R Y   S I D
T O P P E R   A L C A P P
    S O U N D S G O O D T O M E
B S M T   P A T   D A T E S
Y E A H   A R T   A S S N S
```

10

```
OMEGA█FACTS█CHOSE
HAVEL█TREAT█LULUS
GRITS█KENNYROGERS
OTTO█GNATS█OTOOLE
DIANAROSS█SCH█SYN
███LAX███TAKEI██
BALLAD█RAINY█STLO
ATEAM█SERGEI█HOAR
THEPOINTERSISTERS
HODS█MEANIT█LARGO
ELSE█SEPTS█WARREN
██SPORE███HIP███
PBS█IRS██PAULSIMON
IRATER█TARDY█PERI
QUINCYJONES█HARDG
UNDUE█ADANO█UNTIE
ETATS█ROMAN█HAZEL
```

15

```
GOOD█GUMM██ABBA
ANDI█ISEE█GAUL
STOCKSANDBONDS█
PORKY█TOIL█SCAM
██TRIO█CUR█OCT
BEERANDWINE█LEN
LAVA█FAO█TAIL
TRACT█YRS█PSYCH
██NYET█LTR█LEAR
AAH█CREDITCARDS
FLU█HIT█NEON██
LAND█THUG█ODDER
██STOLENPROPERTY
█KEMP█ISAK█RATA
█ARES█CAYS█STAN
```

64